PENGUIN BOOKS
SUPERPOWERS ON THE SHORE

Sejal Mehta is a journalist and editor. She has worked in, and written for, the magazine and newspaper industry for the past twenty years, including for *Lonely Planet Magazine India*, *National Geographic Traveller India* and Nature inFocus. She is also a published author of children's books.

For the last seven years, Sejal has walked across shores in India with the team of Marine Life of Mumbai, a citizen-led initiative, documenting and creating awareness about the city's coastal biodiversity. Her forte has become making science palatable and fun for lay readers. Through her conversations about the intertidal zone with adults and children over the years, she has found an engaged audience, ready to convert to tide pooling on their own.

PRAISE FOR THE BOOK

'How often would you come across references to pop culture, children's literature, comic books, and even Sridevi and Bollywood in a book about the environment? Our answer would be none. Presented in a quirky and engaging style, the book will intrigue even those readers who might not typically be drawn towards learning about nature around us, let alone India's marine life, and the cool, really important roles that sea creatures play in this ecosystem . . . Aided by Jessica Luis' delightful illustrations and content that is presented in a quirky and engaging style, the book will intrigue even those readers, who might not be typically drawn towards learning about nature around us, let alone marine life'—*Mid-Day*

'Through experiences from her travels, interviews with experts, research findings, and pop-culture references, the book shapes an introduction to weird and wonderful marine creatures, and the beautiful moments and deadly battles that play out in the intertidal zone'—***Condé Nast Traveller India***

'This is a simply bewitching, scintillating little book, which I shall probably read and re-read till I know it by heart. The back flap describes Mehta as a "journalist and editor" who has worked for *Lonely Planet, National Geographic Traveller India* etc. and has written fiction for children. What it doesn't mention is that she has an irrepressible, incorrigible sense of humour that most lead-footed "science writers" would be shocked by. All our leaden, heavyweight deadly dull textbooks ought to be written this way'—***Open***

'What *Superpowers on the Shore* does is make you think about the resilience of creatures that otherwise do not get enough attention. [Mehta's] writing in the book is an engaging mix of pop culture, science and keen observations. It is a style of writing that also makes the book easy to understand, even for casual readers who might not be that interested in the environment and conservation'—***Mint Lounge***

'*Superpowers on the Shore* explores [the] unusual life in intertidal pools. It's a pop-science work for adults, kept relatable and fun. It is an unusual approach, even for a work on pop science. But it succeeds in making this almost alien world accessible to the reader'—***Hindustan Times***

'In the chapter called "Walking – an exercise in seeing" from a book on the creatures that populate India's intertidal zone, the author ruminates on the things an individual can learn about herself and the world during a walk on the beach'—***Hindustan Times***

'This is an unusual book in that the author seems to be rebelling against usual tomes of science writing, which are usually bone dry and superior sounding. Wonder and humility seem to be Mehta's weapons of choice that arbitrate between the mundane and exciting aspects of a coastline (and broadly, of life)'—***Hindustan Times***

'What do you get where sand and sea water, wind and sunlight all come together? A coast, you might say. But this book says it's magic! Interspersed with chapters on the superpowers are smaller chapters on the intertidal environment itself, with simple things to look for and listen for when you happen to be on the beach, where the waves pound the sand in the intertidal zone, where all good things happen. If you have the faintest interest in life forms other than human, or if, like me, you're a beach freak, this is a read you shouldn't miss'—*Deccan Chronicle* and *Asian Age*

'Sejal Mehta, in her book, outlines the rich diversity that stands toe-to-toe with the rich wildlife of the rainforests and ones that have given birth to countless works of fantasy and fiction'—*Daily Star*

'Sejal Mehta has for the last four years walked the shores across India looking for creatures in intertidal zones—spaces explorable upon the retrieval of high tides. By virtue of traversing the sea as well the shores, the life forms found in intertidal spaces are blessed with features that appear otherworldly'—*Down to Earth*

'Sejal Mehta takes us on a journey into the world of marine life, educating us on the fascinating and terrifying creatures that lurk beneath the waves. They survive with interesting abilities like regeneration, defence mechanisms and sonic skills. It is a fascinating and enthralling book that can aid in the study and knowledge of the species that live in our environment. This great novel should be read and marvelled at'—*Frontlist*

'This book made my eyes go wide; right there virtually underfoot was an astonishing, kaleidoscopic world crammed with the most amazing life and I had missed it all'—*Indian Express*

'The book is about us and the animals, and the lessons their powers teach us, about our own arsenals, our lives and the strengths we possess. And what the tide, with its daily journey back and forth can remind us about ourselves'—**Indiatimes**

'This book about a parallel universe that hides in plain sight, right at the shore, has a secret message: Everybody can be a scientist or an explorer'—**Roundglass Sustain**

'What fascinated me was the multifaceted experience of having one's attention dragged hither and thither, between prose and poetry, conversations and lectures, now dealing with the predilections of the particular creature under examination, then musings of the author interspersed with resonating quotes from other authors, and much more, all told with excitement. For me, this was very different fare to what I have been used to.

Science abhors emotion, but by dint of objective observation, scientists find out stories about creatures that can titillate the imagination, if told in a lively manner. I appreciated the emotional way, in which the observations of scientists, familiar to me as a specialist, are related to an audience of interested onlookers. It's like making bland western food into chatpata chaat. The Bollywood song-and-dance interjections are incorporated here as well. For me, the book is very feminine, very Indian, in a very appealing manner'—*India Today*

'Sejal Mehta's book opens up the rich and fascinating world of intertidal organisms to anyone with the inclination to pause and look at what a receding tide reveals. Day or night, this zone can thrill you with its inhabitants, be it an unexpected octopus on a Mumbai beach or the glowing plankton in the tidal pools of a rural coastline. There is much beauty, drama, and resilience in the beings of this zone, so diverse in form and function. A walk along the beach may never be the same again once you have read *Superpowers on the Shore*'—**Jury citation, Green Literature Festival Honour Book Awards 2023**

'If you're a beach person, this is the perfect book to pick up before you plan your next seaside holiday. Sejal Mehta offers a bewitching—and often hilarious—window to the fascinating biodiversity that thrives unnoticed in innocuous tide pools. From penis-fencing flatworms to home-swapping hermit crabs and camouflaging cephalopods, there's a lot going on in those pools that reveal themselves during low tide. You just have to know where to look and what to look for—this book will help'—*Harper's Bazaar*

'Sejal Mehta wandered around India's intertidal zones and has written a lovely book about odd and adorable marine creatures. I urge you to please read it'—**Bahar Dutt, journalist and author**

'This book nudges you to take a walk along the seashore, across tide pools and explore the living world therein. Avoiding too much jargon, and yet scientific in approach, Sejal Mehta fetches stories from her deep memory, invests her imagination and creates a fascinating palette of the lives of the denizens of the intertidal zone.

Interspersed with many poems and ending with "letters"— purportedly from some of these amazing animals; each one of these is a pedagogical method to engage with bored students rather than stuff them with facts. In the end, she flips the "superpower concept" and leaves us with a sense of purpose by posing the question, "Are we not superpowers too? We have it in us to save nature and the intertidal belt in particular?" For if not us, who will? Each illustration, drawn superbly by Jessica Luis, is a creative story in itself'—**Ravindranath G., teacher of zoology, Royal College of Arts, Science and Commerce, Maharashtra**

SUPERPOWERS ON THE SHORE

SEJAL MEHTA

PENGUIN BOOKS

An imprint of Penguin Random House

PENGUIN BOOKS

Penguin Books is an imprint of the Penguin Random House group of companies whose addresses can be found at global.penguinrandomhouse.com

Published by Penguin Random House India Pvt. Ltd
4th Floor, Capital Tower 1, MG Road,
Gurugram 122 002, Haryana, India

Penguin
Random House
India

First published in Viking by Penguin Random House India 2022
This edition published in Penguin Books 2025

ISBN 9780143475194

Typeset in Paciencia by Manipal Technologies Limited, Manipal
Printed at Gopsons Papers Pvt. Ltd., Noida

www.penguin.co.in

100%
Paper from well-
managed forests
FSC   FSC® C191020

*To my father, who would have loved
this book no matter what was inside it*

&

*For coasts everywhere, and the shore
friendships you and I are yet to make*

CONTENTS

You and I

Hi. Listen, did you know?
A sea star can eject its stomach while eating
Goby fish and shrimp have a room-mate agreement
Sea snails have teeth on their tongues!
Oh, you don't like snails?
Don't worry about it, you can meet the octopuses.
Or watch the egrets take flight.
Or you can just sit and watch the ocean awhile
And follow the high drama in the sunset skies.
Rest here.
You don't have to agree with me.
I'd prefer it if you didn't sometimes.
You might not like the ocean
I might find the city stifling.
But perhaps you can tell me how you find city lights comforting
And I can confess how the sea reminds me of my father
We can share the best parts about these spaces
And file them away, so we can tell someone else.
To better navigate them
A like-minded group is good
The opposite, perhaps even better.
Isn't this how we remember things?
Isn't this how we find support?
Isn't this how we survive
And perhaps save ourselves from ruin?
Isn't this how a community builds?
With a simple, hi, did you know?

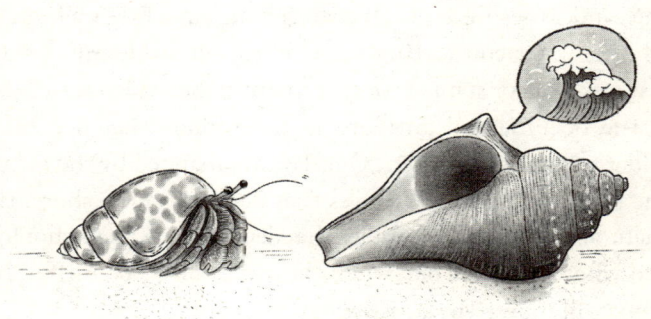

INTRODUCTION
A SUPERHERO UNIVERSE

R oar.
 That is the sound the ocean makes when its waves break against the shore.

Do you hear it?

Imagine a wave that gradually builds in the ocean, forming a swell on the surface of the water. It rises up and out, higher and higher until the shallows cause it to topple and crash against the shore, shattering into a foamy mix of sand, rock and salt water.

A single roar that has enlisted the powers of wind and gravity.

Pull back.

Repeat.

For people living by the coast, it is this sound that permeates our consciousness. It's a sound that allows us pause, delight, comfort. It's a sound that we escape to, it accompanies our morning jogs and our romantic strolls, and it forms a backdrop to the sandcastles we build. It accompanies us as we walk on the beach, the water comfortingly encircling our ankles. It's a sound that serves as a constant accompaniment to our video travelogues. It is the documented antidote to the sounds that our brains consider to be threat triggers. Our days are mapped by the turning of the tides: for the human lives that depend on the shore, they are natural clocks with schedules that decide when boats should be pulled ashore or rowed out, when the catch will be bountiful, how currents will move. The tides are our allies.

India's 7,500 kilometres of coastline runs across different landscapes, cities, towns and villages, changing its outfits for different destinations as it travels: sandy stretches on some beaches of Goa, rocky patches and jagged cliff faces in Karwar, the sentinel mangrove forests of the Sunderbans.

Do you see it?

It tells different stories at each of these shores, and enables diverse protagonists to live their coastal lives. It ensures that no two shores are the same.

Our coasts are portals to another world. Think back to the last time you visited a shore. The way to it could be through a village, next to a row of buildings, or along forest paths that lead to sandy beaches. If you're in a city like Mumbai, you merely run screaming off of a cacophonous street. One minute you're crossing a busy road, navigating the traffic with the determined talent of a video game character — hand held out to the honking drivers — and the next, you've walked right into Wakanda.* If you are used to your line of sight constantly being obstructed by buildings, cars, trains

---

* Wakanda is a fictional country in East Africa appearing in American comic books published by Marvel Comics. Created by Stan Lee and Jack Kirby.

and people, the suddenness of a vast ocean, which stretches as far as the eye can see, is a sanctuary. The shades of blue, the enveloping softness of the sand and the idea of standing on the edge of something so unfathomably limitless is disorientating and deeply satisfying, all at once.

When I was a child, my father told me to align myself with the sea if I ever lost track of directions. I never forgot it. On journalism assignments, I mapped my routes keeping the closest waterbody as my frame of reference, be it a river, a lake, or an oceanfront.

For children from coastal areas, our childhood memories are dotted with sand and surf: family outings, morning picnics, the sweet taste of coconut water and the consequent mystery of how much and how soft the *malai* is, and the buttery or sickeningly sweet delights of the shops on the shore. The people who visit are all stories, each person a tale themselves.

During the legendary Mumbai monsoons, while the city scurried indoors from the onslaught, my father would take me to the beach at Juhu. The rain in Mumbai is determined, hard-working and torrential, much like its citizens. In June, I imagine that rain clouds arrive in the city, unpack their bags, lease housing for the next four months, delegate areas of operations, set up thunderous background scores and ready themselves for the intensity that their task demands. The Mumbai monsoon meant business, and I was here for it. We would form a human chain, sometimes my dad, my brother and I, sometimes a laughing gang of six to seven cousins, all standing thigh-deep or ankle-deep in water, depending on how safe it was, holding hands and laughing until our sides hurt as the waves crashed at us and stole our chappals. The rain pelted resolutely on us, challenged by this audacious, motley crew that dared to step out in the deluge.

Among all the memories I have possessively saved of my father, whom I lost to a sudden and fatal heart attack, the sound of his delighted laughter and firm grip on my tiny hand, telling me he'd always ensure I was safe, remain etched in every corner of my brain.

The coast is a gift. It knows.

It's also the way that water makes us feel. Water falling from the sky, water skipping down a mountain, crashing into a valley, water flowing in a stream. Why do so many people use the sound of the ocean to sleep? The answer is acoustic camouflage. 'Non-threatening noises can drown out those sounds that might otherwise raise red flags in the brain's threat-activated vigilance system', said Orfeu Buxton, an associate professor of bio-behavioural health at Pennsylvania State University at the time, who had conducted a study in a hospital on sleep patterns and the effect that sound plays on sleep. The study aimed to facilitate improving care for patients of acoustic assault. Our brains are wired to react to sudden sounds, like a scream or a piercing alarm more so than the noise of traffic or flowing water, with a stress response. According to a quote in Live Science, Buxton said, 'These slow, whooshing noises are the sounds of non-threats, which is why they work to calm people . . . It's like they're saying: "Don't worry, don't worry, don't worry".'

As this beautiful extract from Maria Popova's brilliant newsletter, *The Marginalian*, formerly known as *Brain Pickings*, says:

> But where does the modern soul go to pasture on awareness and commune with the cosmos in a civilization increasingly savaged by noise? Where do we find, and how do we protect, those places where, in the lovely words of the poet Wendell Berry, 'one's inner

voices become audible [and,] in consequence, one responds more clearly to other lives'?

It is ironic that the all-consuming roar of the sea stands guard at the portal, politely telling the sounds of the city to 'please find something else to do while you're here'.

An intertidal zone is a part of the place where the land meets the sea—it is the portion of our shore that is covered by water at high tide and is revealed at low tide. On the one hand, we have the extreme life of the deep sea, and on the other, human settlement. In the middle is this space that is accessible on foot only at low tide. While this interplay of the submergence and emergence of land is a shared one, humans don't have free rein—we venture in on foot only when the water recedes, and the turning of the tide signals that we have overstayed our welcome, provoking an insatiable curiosity about its functioning. It is a bit like the poet Rumi's proverbial field between right and wrong, but without all the emotional turbulence.

And it is this part that forms the foundation of our story.

Because here be superpowers: venomous assassins, shapeshifting molluscs and regenerative worms.

For superpowers to exist, it stands to reason that there must be a universe that facilitates it.

People, it's a damn superhero kingdom.

To be honest, the only reason I stepped onto a shore to look for animals four years ago was because I thought some marine biologists had collectively lost their marbles.

I had moved to Bangalore from Mumbai for a few years for work (I was an editor at a magazine there), and I'd heard rumblings about a trio called 'Marine Life of Mumbai' (MLOM) doing wildlife walks (aka nature trails) on our shores back home.

Having grown up in Mumbai, this was perplexing to me on many levels. There were more people at the touristy waterfront at Bandra Bandstand on any given day than at a Beyoncé Knowles concert. How could any animals stand for that sort of thing, not just in Mumbai, but anywhere?

The claim that wildlife flourished on Mumbai's polluted shores was preposterous to me.

These biologists were surely disproportionately excited about a few crabs. So when I visited the city, I went for a walk with Abhishek Jamalabad, a marine biologist and one of the founders of the collective, confident that I would return underwhelmed.

Readers, humble pie tastes positively revolting.

The first walk was at the iconic Haji Ali dargah, that too on a monsoon morning. When we see the structure from the road, few of us know what lies beyond the structure—a rocky coastline that is open at low tide, with boulders and rocks and pebbles, and creatures. I was overwhelmed by tiny animals that were stoically going about their morning rituals. I met hermit crabs, barnacles and oysters, and was bamboozled by the idea that all around the world, where land meets the sea, an entire civilization full of exciting creatures was waiting to be met.

I walked around the shore as the rain clouds gathered. Soon, it started showering down on us. Both animals and humans scurried for cover, the latter in a far less elegant manner over the slippery rocks. Later, huddled under a makeshift shelter, with chai in hand, and the monsoon purging my tired city heart, we talked about the intertidal zone—this strange space between land and sea—and thus began a relationship with the coast.

Four years later, after hundreds of outings to different shores in my waterproof shoes (yes, I have those now), and torturing myself with science papers and interviews with scientists, I write to tell you, readers, that our shorelines are literally crawling and brimming with wildlife. It seems unfathomable to me how the simple act of walking on a seashore can be this vital, that the shore I grew up near, and other countless shores elsewhere, are littered with stories and characters yet untold.

I know this place. I've spent time here. I am a familiar.

Having said that, does this book have everything you need to know about the intertidal creatures? No.

Does it include ALL the animals with ALL their superpowers? Of course not. There's so much yet to see and discover. I mean, scientists might still be discovering fragments of continents, so what are we even talking about?

Is this a book about fisheries at the intertidal zones? No.

I can see you wondering why you've picked this up by now.

Okay, here's what it's about.

These are a handful of my observations of the animals that I have met in the four years I have been walking around in the intertidal zones. It's basically a place for you to start, and somewhere, a place for me to examine what I now know. What has the exploration meant? It's meant that I am aware that a forest lies at the peripheries of our immediate consciousness. It just looks a little different from the forests that we are used to. It's meant that I have new animals to introduce to your heart.

We delight in the high tide as it comes bounding across from the sea, pouring over rocks and flowing purposefully towards the beach line. We like a full, roaring beach. It's a gorgeous spectacle. But something powerful happens at low tide too. As the water withdraws back into itself, spent after its fervent pummelling of the shore, it pulls the veil back on a secret universe, filled with beings possessing higher powers.

I have attributed what we understand about them to superpowers, although in the animals' book, it's a day in their lives; they're not actually the Avengers.

These are the creatures of the intertidal zone. As the tide retreats, this universe allows us a glimpse of its animals — crabs, sea snails, eels, and so many more — performing duties, building households and connections, only with their superpowers. Through this book, we will meet some of these animals and see for ourselves how these superpowers lend themselves to a life on our shores.

But why would these animals need powers?

Think about every superhero phenomenon you've ever come across. The rise of the 'superpower' occurred sometime in the early 1900s, and it reflected the socio-economic state of society at the time. A hero always came alive in the face of adversity. This was presented to the larger society in various forms: oppression, bullying, tyranny, crime, and demonic antagonists. A hero (or many heroes) would then rise to stabilize the world.

There's one important distinction here. Nature has no evil intent. The intertidal zone is a harsh place only because of how it is placed in the ecosystem.

Consider these circumstances for a home: a stretch of land exposed to harsh sunlight and cool moonlight, facing the continuous ebb and flow of saline water; a place that has different predators and threats from both the shallows and the land; and finally, the endless daily construction of the homes — they are built only to be taken down by the water, and then constructed yet again.

An endless state of transience.

Rebecca Helm, an assistant professor at the University of North Carolina, Asheville, navigates complex science through her outreach. She conducts science communication on her website, but she engages readers and breaks down science concepts in conversations on social media with grace and ease. Her eagerness to share her learning and educate, inform and delight while doing so has won her a strong following. She describes the intertidal space as a:

> ... unique community of creatures that can tolerate both air and water exposure. Often, these creatures are much tougher than creatures that live only in the open ocean or deep-sea: intertidal creatures must contend with constant change, only those creatures most flexible survive well here!

Nowhere else—not in the deep seas, nor in the forests—do these specific conditions affect the inhabitants in this way. And the best of these explorations take place during spring tides, which are around the new or full moon. What does it mean to say, it's a good tide to go tidepooling? Don't low tides occur every day? Yes, a good tide (in Mumbai) is anything lower than 0.5 metres on the tide chart, but this depends on the shore, and where the water retreats and how much. On certain shores in Gujarat, the water retreats way inwards every day. So, walk the intertidal zone irrespective, just know that documentation gets better as tides get lower.

I am often asked questions along the lines of 'how do I get closer to nature', 'how do I write about nature', 'how can I help the environment', 'where do I fit in', 'do I have to conserve nature to enjoy it', 'do I need to travel to forests', and 'how do I get my children to respect nature'.

This isn't a popular opinion, but I don't believe that there is one correct way to fall in love with the wilderness. I would go so far as to say that you need not fall in love with it (spoiler alert: you will, though). You just need to engage with it and spare a thought about how it lives. I started with the big moments, my heart only concerned about big cats and larger mammals like elephants. As I looked closer, my love expanded to include the little things, like the wildlife next to my house at the time. And the book I chose to write is about the 'invisible' shore life, some of whom would fit on my little fingertips.

Just be interested.

How? In this book, the Juhu beach makes multiple appearances. It's not that it has the most diversity or the most accurate representation of an intertidal zone; no, it's because it is my patch.

What does that mean?

I attended a talk by a naturalist and birdwatcher, Ramit Singal, at the Karnataka Bird Festival in 2018, where he suggested 'patch birding' to the audience. He encouraged the idea of picking a space near your home and getting to know it better. He was referring to the activity of exploration in terms of birds, but I would use that everywhere. It could be a beach, a park, or your garden. Find a patch, he said, and make that your little wilderness of exploration.

I have more than one patch: Juhu beach, a park where I occasionally run, and the tree opposite my house that has become a roosting site for flying foxes (the greater Indian Fruit fruit bat aka *Pteropus medius*). I don't have to immediately worry about the conservation status of bats or the species of trees in that park or the health of the oceans. I just have to observe my patch. And I did. The patch in the garden nudged me towards changing seasons, how the trees (and, as a result, what lives in them) adapt and look. As I began a determinedly one-sided friendship with the bats, I read about their extreme urban habitat, their midwife care concepts and their colony systems. As I walked at Juhu beach, I understood tides, I watched people engage with the ocean and I noticed the different methods that the fishers use. If you live in a place like Mumbai, the daily marathon from morning to evening and the struggle of this busy, beautiful, tired city makes you tunnel-visioned. You forget about the ocean if you don't actively engage with it for your basic survival.

I have turned cautious as I get older; you can't rush me. From impulsively jumping off every cliff, to now testing the waters obsessively, I am a case study in self-preservation. Four years ago, as I gingerly stepped onto the intertidal zone, despite a fair bit of excitement, true to character, I waited at the periphery, watching the others go down on their hands and knees, moving rocks aside and peering into crevices. I was re-piecing myself from a difficult life event, and in the classic way that people who have their defences boarded up as high as the cliffs surrounding the beaches in Karwar, Karnataka, I took my time committing to the coast. I watched — it's okay, I am just looking, I am a writer, just passing through — as the biologists embraced tide cycles and spring tides, and brought books on identification. The self-preservation tribe in my reader group will know what I mean, yes? Yes. High five to y'all too.

Intimidated by the level of fast-growing expertise in the team, I didn't bother with identification and just stood and watched the sunset instead, had conversations with the fishers, dug my heels in the sand (refreshing to do it literally for once), and waited for others to show me what they'd find.

And that was just fine.

Slowly, perhaps like some of the animals that move along the intertidal spaces, I kept pace with the ways of discovery. First, I turned my attention to the shorefronts, and how different they are. Have you noticed this? How the water behaves with the breaking of waves on different shores. Have you noticed when the tide turns? It's very forceful. Then, I moved on to the animals. I learnt the names of the creatures I favoured, and then the names of the ones that I had been silly enough to overlook. I still haven't become friends with some of them. And that's okay as well.

In 2020 – 21, we were all locked indoors, and I started to see stories of how nature was healing and reclaiming our world. This point of view was worrying. Because, if we are to be locked in indefinitely for nature to thrive, then this is not great news, is it? Perhaps, yes, we gave our surroundings a breather, and perhaps that's part of learning. To coexist, we'll need to be inclusive, make space for both us and the wilderness to breathe. We have lived together for civilizations, so let's stop hogging all the toys for ourselves.

There are innumerable reasons to be interested in the wild. You can choose to say hello to a beautiful creature, or understand how the moon affects our oceans, or you can choose to immerse yourself. I borrow from a story I wrote for *Roundglass Sustain* to provide an answer: when you start watching wildlife in your backyard, you develop an empathy that years of travelling in the wilderness might not yield. You feel a kinship with the creatures that are breathing the same polluted air, living in the same filth, and are subject to the same high decibel levels as you are. You'll see them as citizens of the same locale, just like you. And while you keep checking on the upkeep of your patch, you might wonder about the neighbouring one, and the one beyond that. Maybe the entire city becomes your patch. Imagine how much thought and concern you will invest in ensuring its health. Now, imagine many more of you. Maybe we'll start to treat our backyards better because wild things are wild things, and it really doesn't matter where they live.

But it's been a tough line to toe—conveying the science in this book and yet ensuring that you have fun reading it. Of the two strands, I have chosen the reader that is not yet hooked, not yet aware, not yet immersed. To the scientists whom I've had the pleasure of interacting with, this book is not for you. It's for you to gift to the people in your life who wonder what in the name of god you are doing 'on field' all day. It's to spread the magic you and I have had the pleasure of experiencing.

Despite all its gifts, it's easy to take the shore for granted. The sea is constant and familiar, too familiar perhaps, in the way a family member is. You stop looking at their magic after a while, but it's there all the same. It's the truth of a superpower that it operates in plain sight—a bit like wizards among muggles, or Superman and Clark Kent. If we're looking for secrets, we have to gaze and go closer.

In that, in three years, in a city with high-rises and towers that aspire for the skies, the miniature life of the intertidal areas has brought me, quite literally, to my knees. When the ocean retreats, it leaves behind little pools of water on a rocky shore. These pools are like neighbourhoods. The animals that live here fight for space, and probably have a *nukkad* for evening hang-outs and perhaps even a quintessential cantankerous neighbour who hates everything. At the risk of humanizing their spaces, these are legitimate homes. And if you look even closer, even the animals themselves play hosts—eggs live on shells, sea snails on sea sponges, and so on. There are so many living, breathing homes.

Like the ocean, the intertidal zone is a remnant of what once was. The sand, that we so casually walk on is, in part, a result of changes on the coast over time—rocks that broke down over millions of years, minerals that were left behind, microorganisms like foraminifera, seashells, diatoms and coral rubble. The sand holds evidence of death: the remains of an animal, fossils, bones, and even their poop. Whales, the giants of the deep, are occasionally stranded here, left to a mysterious death that humans then try to place in context. The same happens to turtles, dolphins and porpoises, and so many others, too. The tide pools that form around the boulders (which were left behind by tectonic changes), volcanoes and earthquakes, as the earth shook and raged since the dawn of time and settled into what it is today—our natural spaces are secret keepers of all of that.

When you visit the intertidal zones, you're walking along pages and pages of history, aren't you?

This, then, is the superhero kingdom.

Now, let's go see some powers.

I do have to warn you. The intertidal space is addictive. If you're like me, there will come a time when you can't watch a Bollywood beach scene without wondering what's living under those rocks. It's a bloody nightmare. All that I said earlier, about water pushing you toward introspection—these are not light warnings. Walk a few steps and you should be on full alert for epiphanies, locked-away memories or an inexplicable desire to write a poem or create something else. It will trap you into facing your demons, to learn from nature and create a weird urge to become an all-round better human being without ever having the slightest intention to do so.

It's a damn minefield.

Brace yourselves.

For now, put on your waterproof shoes. Carry drinking water, and a hat and a torch.

I am delighted I have you for company.

Come, let's begin.

I have someone I'd like you to meet.

~

Hermit Crab pushes through the crowd.

The tiny dead fish lay at the foot of a large pebble.

How absolutely crowded this neighbourhood is now, she thinks.

Maybe she should look for other restaurants. The tide pool near the sunset point rock face looked interesting, and yet less populated. She will try that tomorrow.

She shoulders another crab and tries to get to the dead fish.

Someone's shell gets her in the eye. 'OW! WATCH IT!'

'See then, where you're going, no!' the other crab is already nibbling at the fish.

Hermit Crab pushes behind as a sea of others yell and move around her,

all attempting to eat various parts of the fish.

She squares her shell, frowns determinedly and charges over a few bodies to reach the fish.

The others protest. 'CAN YOU PLEASE NOT! THERE IS NO PLACE!'

Hermit Crab is unfazed. 'Arre, uncle, fourth seat place is there, above.'

She catapults her way up and reaches the slightly raised rock above.

She starts to feed from that vantage point.

Below her, a fight breaks out. In the chaos, she can't tell whether they're squabbling over a new shell or food. She recognizes some of the street gang. She is glad she moved up earlier. She continues to feed while keeping one eye on the fight and cringes when one literally rips out another's limbs from under his shell.

Brutal and impressive all at once, she thinks.

Very Satya or Godfather, whichever way you want to look at it.

Every few minutes, someone knocks at her shell, or attempts to
  dislodge her, at one point she is literally eating upside down.
  But she hangs on.
That's how you get by here.
Survival of the pushiest.

~

How many of you thought of crowded local trains? Mumbaikars, I see you.

There's a creature that I resonate with. If I had to pick a mascot for the intertidal zone, I'd select the hermit crab.

A hermit crab's life is a tough one. It's called a crab, but it isn't a 'true crab' in a scientific sense. Unlike most crabs, it has no hard carapace covering its entire body, but a soft, slightly lopsided abdomen. It is vulnerable to desiccation by the harsh sun, and predators. So, it literally has to acquire shells that have been left behind by dead sea snails and wear them as a mobile home. When you meet one, it'll most likely be staggering across the shore, wearing someone else's shell. Now you see where the name comes from. At some point, they outgrow these shells and will have to start the tedious process of finding new, bigger shells. A bigger, better real estate possibility is always on the horizon for this fellow.

How Mumbai can you possibly get?

I've observed hermit crabs improvise in the absence of shells (PSA: don't pick shells up from the shore, people, leave them for the hermit crabs. Otherwise, you're causing a property imbalance in their real estate market!). They'll use bottle caps, trash and even empty tequila glasses. These are probably the first animals you'll learn to recognize. They're of different sizes and need shells that fit. Watch how they move to identify them. They scuttle along;

they won't smoothly glide like the original owner of the shell. I met my first hermit crab on Carter's Road in Mumbai, and sat and watched a huge specimen literally come out of its shell. Literally. Not as a metaphor to meet other crabs or anything.

Some terrestrial or land hermit crabs from the Andaman Islands engage in an orderly network for house hunting. Land hermits are able to breathe outside water and stay almost entirely on land with close access to the ocean. The adorable hermit crabs from the Andaman Islands queue up for empty shells. When an empty shell is spotted, it's like any self-respecting real estate network. The word spreads, and everyone knows a new apartment is suddenly available. Hermit crabs will come to the shell for inspection. They'll try the shell out, and if it doesn't suit their needs, they'll all wait until another crab picks it up because then, the new tenant's old home will be discarded, and might be of interest to the others. And so it goes. A trial queue of homes that fit and homes that don't feel right and those that do.

Also, imagine a crab that lives on trees! Robber crabs (because they steal coconuts and break them open using their sheer strength) or coconut crabs are terrestrial hermit crabs found in the Nicobar Islands. When they are young, they hustle for shells the same way marine hermits do. They have the additional ability to shape their limbs into a door that snugly fits the opening of the shell, to conserve moisture in their terrestrial lifestyle. They have specialized organs known as branchiostegal lungs to help them breathe on land. When they're older, they discard them and hulk it through life without any need for protection. And they do so with good reason — they can grow up to 1 metre and are sometimes 4 kilograms in weight! Some are actually known to hunt birds and rats! Imagine a crab eating a bird. Apologies for that terrifying visual.

It's fair to say that their populations are massive — they are present all across the coast. There hasn't been a shore I haven't seen them on, and in huge numbers. And I have to say, shell exchange is not always an orderly operation among all species. On more than one occasion, we've seen hermits actually fighting with each other for space, although there is a method to that madness too. Once, we spotted a crab kicking an individual off when it was on top of a hydroid, sending it swinging while it was clutching onto the stalk for dear life. Another time, a few crabs got into a fight for a shell that might become the envy of the neighbourhood.

I am going to use the help of this not-a-true-crab to take you through parts of the book. We'll watch her go through some of her tide pool haunts and glimpse her friends through her life.

First stop: invisibility.

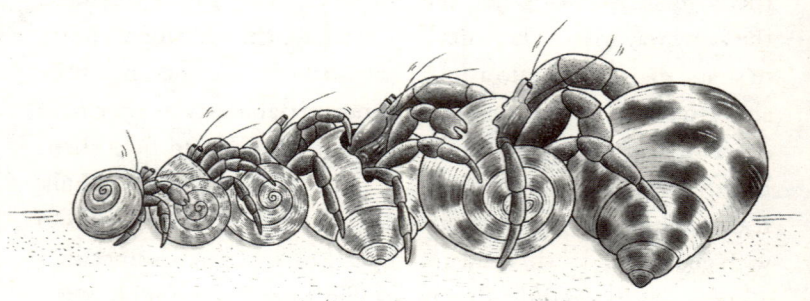

A housing shell exchange line-up by hermit crabs

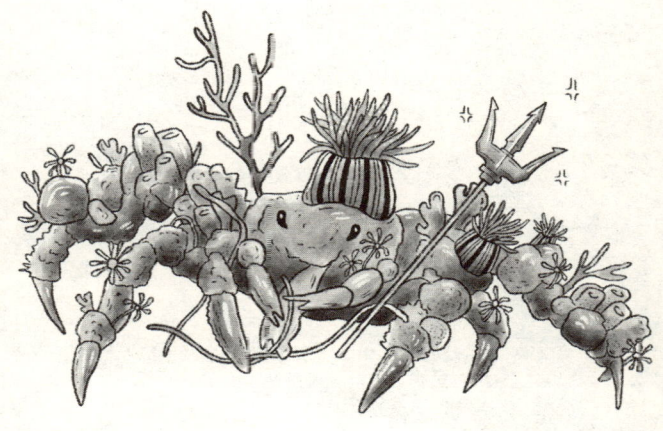

THE POWER OF INVISIBILITY

CAMOUFLAGE AND THE CHANGING SELF

I don't know why people are so keen to put the details of their private life in public; they forget that invisibility is a superpower.

— Banksy

In 2001, the superpower experiment took the Internet by storm. The popular podcast *This American Life* asked listeners to pick between the power to fly or be invisible. The experiment has since been used numerous times, notably in *Psychology Today* and *Forbes* magazines.

Cephalopods at work: (From top) Octopus, squid and cuttlefish with their
invisibility cloaks

The rules were laid out—you could only pick one and both had limitations. You could fly at 1,00,000 feet, at a maximum velocity of 1000 kilometres/hour. Invisibility would allow you to be unseen, along with your clothes and everything else, but what you picked up or ate (until digested) was visible.

Obviously, you have questions. The test anticipated it. No, you have no additional powers: no superhuman strength to carry anyone else, no abilities to pass through walls or open doors.

The results for this experiment then (and a casual survey done by me for this chapter) showed how differently humans and animals might use powers had they both been picked from the evolutionary line-up to have them. Humans obviously came up short; otherwise, production houses would be earning millions not from Superman, but the occasional normalcy of the average Joe.

What would you pick? Think about it and I will come back to this a little later.

Dressmakers and Dapper Hatters: Camouflage but in Style

Hermit Crab and Sea Urchin step into a store
It's one of those classy joints, you know, like Halston's line.
(You've already met the hermit crab.
To imagine the sea urchin, think of a ball with spines all over.)
Sea Urchin starts to browse. Summer is almost here, so he was
  looking forward to new collections.
He tries on a traditional wide-brimmed hat; it sits jauntily on
  his spikes
Hermit Crab considers him critically, 'Hmm, perhaps when
  sunbathing at a tide pool,' she says. 'How about this?' She
  hands him an ocean blue beanie.

Sea Urchin makes a face. 'Does nothing for my shape, that hat. Actually, very few heads are blessed for that gear.'

Hermit Crab puts it back and spies something on the rock table. 'Oh, but what's that?'

Her eye falls on a dry rust leaf — beautifully preserved.

She reaches out for it and it suddenly moves, and they see it's actually sitting on someone's head.

Hermit Crab recoils in shock.

The owner of the store, Decorator Crab, looks up from her ledger.

She has bits and pieces from the store all over her, but in a way that fits.

Hermit Crab and Sea Urchin stare at her in awe. 'Oh, I am sorry, we didn't see you there at all.'

Hermit Crab stammers, 'W-we're looking for a hat for Sea Urchin here.'

Decorator Crab looks the sea urchin up and down in an interested yet uninterested manner,

That only the truly fashionable can pull off.

She pulls out more dried leaves — colourful and contoured — from under a rock.

'New line. Organic, and sustainable hats,' the crab drawls, 'Made locally, no less.'

Sea Urchin tries one on. Slightly less protection than a shell, but quite the chic statement.

'I'll take one in every summer colour,' he says.

~

On the shores of Alibag, I met a rather dapper sea urchin. I'd met other individuals before, bobbing back and forth with the waves in Karwar, Karnataka's spectacular intertidal region. I was strongly reminded of those martial arts weapons with a chain and a ball with spikes; a close parallel is the meteor hammer weapon Gogo Yubari uses in the movie *Kill Bill: Volume 1*, but that had just one row of spikes. The sea urchin is covered with them.

But the urchin likes to accessorize. The one sitting in a tide pool at Akshi beach in Alibag wore a leaf, and another one wore some shells in an attempt to blend into their background. A rather delightful news story made the rounds in April 2020, when a Colorado aquarium enthusiast, Wilson Souza, started making custom sea urchin hats. Emma Verling, who holds a doctorate in marine ecology from University College Cork, described to *Newsweek* how sea urchins mount hats, shells, rocks and other objects atop their spines, manipulating objects with hundreds of tube feet — flexible stalks with suction cups. Wilson Souza's first design was meant to be functional rather than stylish, but since then, he's had to become a fashion designer of sorts for the echinoderms (a phylum including sea urchins, starfish and sea cucumbers), tailoring cowboy, Viking and top hats for aquarium animals. In the wild, of course, that won't do at all. The sea urchin's action is a covering behaviour as part of protection from predators, extreme temperatures and light. Covering behaviour is actually quite common in the intertidal zone. Some carrier snails stick dead shells to their outer surfaces in an attempt to camouflage themselves.

On two occasions, I've mistaken a decorator crab (also called the Velcro crab) for hydroids or seaweed, *while I was peering at it*. I was told, 'Look, its arms are moving side to side.' Bro, it's a tide pool, everything is moving side to side. The decorator crab — part of the superfamily Majoidea, which also hosts spider crabs — is a strange creature, so it immediately ranks very high in my book.

Research has found that about 75 per cent of majoid crab species use a rather startling method to be invisible.

A decorator crab has hook-like hairs on its exoskeleton (the hard outer casing of the body). The hairiness provides the animal with a unique life hack. It uses its pincers, which are short and cylindrical, to cut off bits of sea sponge and seaweed, and 'sticks' them onto itself with the help of the hair. It also picks up seashells and debris. 'The decorator crab is a perfect study example because the Indo-Pacific species has Velcro-like substances on its shell and hooks on its appendages that enable it to secure items on its exterior,' said marine scientist Danielle Dixson, whose team studied its behaviour. Basically, it's not very fussy. Pretty much anything that will allow it to hide is useful.

An interesting species from New Zealand, *Notomithrax ursus* lives among seaweed and uses it for camouflage. But the paper suggests that it be called a 'dressmaker' because it chooses algae that it can measure and cut, passing them to its mouth and then planting them on its body. It also ensures that the severed ends go into the setae, the body, while the intact, smooth ends remain visible. It uses a pattern based on the hooked setae, and produces a garment of sorts to avoid predation. This suggests an evolution from passive to active camouflage. Therefore, not only is it proficient at tailoring, but also has a good eye for finishing.

I know what you're thinking. When Hannibal Lecter* rips off a man's face to prevent detection, we're all screaming bloody murder, but this little fellow is literally walking around with body parts from across its neighbourhood, and we're all going, 'Aw, that is adorable.'

---

* Hannibal Lecter is a fictional character created by novelist Thomas Harris.

Blatant favouritism.

Having said that, if the universe had a favourite, it made no attempt to hide it.

Armed, Invisible and Fabulous: Cephalopod Supremacy

Cephalopods received an entire arsenal of superpowers, favouritism be damned. This group—some of whom feature in this book, like octopuses, squids, cuttlefish and nautiluses—make headlines in popular science articles every week. I had to set a deadline for this book to include new research about what a cephalopod can now do, because otherwise I'd never be done. If, by the time you're reading this, it has been discovered that they can make tea and do the garba, well, there it is.

Seeing an octopus on the shore is a bit like spotting a big cat—you can feel the thrill in the air as everyone gracelessly scampers over slippery surfaces to get to it, knowing full well that there's a good chance it's vanished without a trace by the time they get there.

Usually, crowds at the Juhu beach throng the sandy portions in front of the beach houses and hotels. On the other side (the coast that travels to the southern part of the city), the rocky shore hosts some beautiful wildlife. I'd like to confess that until I started walking with Marine Life of Mumbai, I had no idea that the Juhu beach had a rocky shoreline at all. But then, I had never really known low tide to be a particularly attractive time to visit either.

But somewhere in these tiny tide pools, I saw my first octopus on land. It was white in colour, a bit short of a foot in length—it was almost the size of a puppy. The octopus breathed in through its gills and threw out excess water from the siphon (which is fashioned like a tube) under its head. Its arms unfurled and withdrew periodically, flashing glimpses of the rows of suckers underneath.

An hour passed, the sun began to rein in the day, and while the others moved on to document different things, I sat at a little distance from it, unable to leave this strange animal. The Internet is flooded with photos and videos of octopuses, but they're usually taken on dives or snorkelling excursions. This one, looking back at me, right in the middle of Juhu beach, as polar opposite to a pristine waterfront as can be, seemed almost like an apparition. Over the course of the next three years, I'd realize that octopuses are in fact a common intertidal sight, but the jolt of delight on sighting one never really plateaued. It only grew.

Alien. That's the word most often used to describe cephalopods, There was some controversial research that promoted the possibility of that theory as well.*

Why would Earth not be capable of creating this creature though? They're here, on Earth, sharing this space with us, and there's so much we don't know about them, so while 'alien' could be used as unfamiliar, most scientists understandably cringe at the *E.T.* reference.

Pop culture does propel that conversation, though. Consider their on-screen presence in the genre of science fiction: the aliens in the movie *Arrival*; the characters in *Futurama*; Marvel films; the octopus-faced Davy Jones in *The Pirates of the Caribbean*; and, despite the petal-shaped face of the Demogorgon in *Stranger Things*, there's no denying some very strong cuttlefish vibes from it. Before we ascribed an extra terrestrial character to it, they had

---

* https://www.sciencedirect.com/science/article/pii/S00796107183 00798?via%3Dihub.

already lent themselves to the myth of the sea monsters on the high seas.

On 6 August 1848, the crew of a boat off the African coast spotted a giant squid in the ocean, but described it as a gigantic sea serpent, a monster from the abyss. A piece in the *Smithsonian Magazine* describing the incident says:

> The beast was unlike anything the sailors had seen before. News of the encounter hit the British newspaper *The Times* two months later, telling of the ship's brush with a nearly 100-foot monster that possessed a maw 'full of large jagged teeth . . . sufficiently capacious to admit of a tall man standing upright between them.'

Among other such encounters, in a newspaper account in 1902, a sighting of a creature as large as 35 feet caught the attention of scientists and political figures in Germany for further investigation. A research paper described how at that time, two different world views had begun to collide: a belief in myths and legends versus a scientific view that had begun to spread 'in the last third of the nineteenth century in Central and Western Europe and in the United States. People were "discovering" the ocean as a three-dimensional space, which—contrary to traditional beliefs—was filled with living organisms far into the depths.'

History also describes them as formidable enemies, perhaps causing them harm in the same way *Jaws* introduced a deep-seated fear into our minds. According to research papers, 'In mid-nineteenth-century San Francisco, octopuses were abruptly reinvented as "devil-fish," diabolical sea creatures menacing humans who entered their realm. Simultaneously, metaphorical octopuses began appearing in the press, demonizing a range of phenomena.' Add to this Victor Hugo's terrifying and rampantly inaccurate portrayal of octopuses in his 1866 book, *Toilers of the Sea*, where these creatures and their gigantic tentacles evilly drowned humans and caused mayhem. Today, of course, science has reversed how humans see these incredible creatures. Paul Sangl lyrically writes in his paper titled 'Geographic and Discursive Wanderings of San Francisco's "Evil" Octopuses' that 'Consequently, for nearly half a century San Francisco's "evil" octopuses wandered both as hunter and hunted, between sea and land, between the literal, metaphoric, and mythic, between science, literature and the popular press before fading into the tide of history.'

Why do these creatures seem so other-worldly to us? They are absolutely stunning to look at, of course, and they also have highly complex nervous systems (even their arms have clusters of neurons, effectively meaning that they have brain cells on their arms!) and three hearts that pump blue blood. The fascination with their strange yet appealing appearance is an obvious red herring. It is their ability to 'think' and control their powers that makes them irresistible.

In the intertidal zone, they're exciting to engage with. When I first started to observe tide pools after years of chasing elusive wildlife in forests, I was taken aback by how easy it was to watch intertidal inhabitants. Many (but not all) are small, have eyes inconveniently placed to immediately spot me, and a fair number are sessile (attached to a substrate). So I am now a bit spoilt in my wildlife watching. All I clearly need to do is sit near a tide pool while the wildlife is just going about its business.

But not cephalopods.

They're frustratingly hard to photograph because by the time you've seen one, it has clocked your presence *and* an escape route with impressive haste. One second you see it near a rock, and in the next, it's vanished in a flash of arms and eyes, like a magician. It's this awareness of a superior cognitive ability, that it *sees* you, reacts to you, and hoodwinks you all in a split second that makes it infinitely more interesting to us. It's probably why we react more positively to animals that can understand us — like mammals, tigers, elephants or even dogs at home. There are exceptions, of course, and I confess that I am ready to leave the country and run screaming when a roach tries (and they do repeatedly) to have some sort of a connection with me — an absolutely unnecessary phobia rooted in conditioning and yes, I do hope to grow up someday and overcome it and face one.

But there is a trouble in our haste to bequeath the intelligence tag to the cephalopod species. Aditi Pophale, a PhD student in the Computational Neuroethology Unit at the Okinawa Institute of Science and Technology, has been working on octopus research for five years. She cautions against the generalization of superpowers for all octopus species when there is so much left to discover about them. She deals with different species in her laboratory, and while some seemed content to be in the containers, others were escape artists with significant skill sets. She states, 'Five of us were standing around the tank, looking inside it and while we weren't staring at the octopus, we still didn't spot it escape. We noticed only after it'd gone.' She laughed at the memory of trained researchers losing sight of something right in front of them, and also brings home the point of the variation between how different species behave.

Pophale has had the privileged experience of having actual contact with an octopus. She was out on a fisher boat in the Lakshadweep Islands. The fishers caught one, and she saw its skin reacting to the stress it was under — rapidly changing colour, struggling against his hands. Knowing her branch of study, they handed it to her to hold, and she sat with it for a few moments. After a few moments, its colour changed as it calmed down — from a high contrast shade to a more restful hue — and it stayed wrapped around her arm until she literally peeled it off. 'They are very good at chemosensation', she explains, and added that:

> They can smell chemicals; it's like having a tongue attached to your fingertip, where you can taste everything you touch. I'd read that they could possibly sense your hormones through the thin barrier of the skin. They're also curious, so I think once it sensed that I wasn't going to hurt it, it calmed down and stayed.

I always refer to intelligence when speaking of octopuses. They're not like other animals, I say. But Pophale gently urges me to look beyond a human-centric perspective. 'What we see as intelligence', she says, 'is probably a commonality between species. More than being different from the other animals, perhaps we think they're similar to us. Since their cognitive abilities, even the layout of their eyes, are like ours, we see something of ourselves in them.' We do have an inherent bias for things that are like us. Who is to say that sea snails don't 'see' far more clearly than us, or operate on sensory levels so unfamiliar that we can't even comprehend them?

But we're restricted by our version of the truth.

It's understandable. As Steven Pinker says in *How the Mind Works*:

> One of the many reasons we might not be scientists is that our brains are adapted for fitness, not truth. Sometimes the truth is adaptive, at others it is not. And in our minds, conflict of

interest is inherent to the human condition. We would like to want our versions of the truth, rather than what it is.

The more nuanced argument would be that cephalopods seem relatable in a way that they probably shouldn't be, and that probably gets to the heart of why octopuses are so interesting. We don't share the same habitat, sensations or perceptions. That's why it seems like an alien — something that we should have nothing in common with, but in reality, we do.

Whatever it is, if I had to have a superhero on my team, I'd want an octopus on the contract. There's a sequence in the film, *My Octopus Teacher*, where the animal covers herself in broken and abandoned shells to escape a shark attack. After that, she catapults herself from inside the shark's jaws onto its back, riding the confused creature until she can make a smooth escape. The knowing cephalopod, through her growing trust in the film-maker, uses his presence to hunt prey. Against the backdrop of an astonishingly shallow kelp forest, she displays memory retention, curiosity and a rare connection with the film-maker Craig Foster, and in his beautiful words, 'the incredible creativity to deceive'.

You really can't fit them into a box (literally, too, as chances are that they'd escape); they appear to be misfits in their own extended families as well, which is another relatable quality. They belong to the Mollusca class Cephalopoda. But they don't look like their cousins at all. Other molluscs include sea snails, sea slugs, bivalves — most are shelled invertebrates with a dorsal foot. Cephalopods are all arms, and can be as tiny as 1 centimetre and as large at 30 feet. Some of them have brains the size of a walnut, which is large for an invertebrate.

For example, in a master stroke of problem-solving abilities, cuttlefish have the incredible ability to cross-dress in a crowded, competitive mating ritual. Usually, a bunch of cuttlefish males will vie for a single female's attention, not unlike a *swayamvar* situation or an episode of *The Bachelorette*. In this display of macho exhibitionism, a smaller male cuttlefish might miss out. These smart guys will camouflage themselves to appear like a female in order to sneak past the crowd full of burly males and get an audience with the female fish. It's like a foot in the door that's otherwise crowded with competition. In the documentary called *Kings of Camouflage*, Jesse Purdy, a comparative psychologist, said of cuttlefish, 'It's as close perhaps we're going to get to studying an animal on another planet.'*

It makes sense for these molluscs to have added protection in the form of a higher cognition; they don't have a shell covering them, and pretty much everything feeds on cephalopods, including humans. But how did cephalopods manage to secure their own invisibility cloak?

Cephalopods fire from multiple cylinders to achieve this in varying degrees from species to species. There are four main catalysts — chromatophores, iridophores, papillae and leucophores.

Stay with me — this gets very good, very fast.

First up: chromatophores. These are organs on their bodies that contain pigment sacs, which have red, yellow and brown pigment granules. These sacs have a network of radial muscles, meaning muscles arranged in a circle radiating outwards. These are connected to the brain by a nerve.

When the cephalopod wants to change colour, the brain carries an electrical impulse through the nerve to the muscles that

---

* Writer, director, Gisela Kaufmann, *Kings of Camouflage*, 3 April 2007, documentary: 2006 Nova/ PBS documentary.

expand outwards, pulling open the sacs to display the colours on the skin.

Why these three colours? Because these are the colours the light reflects at the depths they live in (the rest is absorbed before it reaches those depths).

On a walk in Juhu, an octopus expertly crawled over from pool to pool and all but galloped towards the approaching tide. On the way, it began flashing brown and white, its skin appearing to dance with colour as it dived into the shallows. As we saw it zoom away using jet propulsion for speed, its colour had changed entirely into brown.

I was gobsmacked. These were the chromatophores at work. You'll see evidence of these even on dead animals that have been stranded on the shore.

Well, what about other colours? Cue the iridophores.

Think of a second level of skin that has thin stacks of cells. These can reflect light back at different wavelengths. Let me make this easier with a few examples. It's using the same properties that we've seen in hologram stickers, or rainbows on puddles of oil. You move your head and you see a different colour. The sticker isn't doing anything but reflecting light—it's your movement that's changing the appearance of the colour. This property of holograms, oil and other such surfaces is called 'iridescence'.

While the chromatophores *actively* achieve colour changes in the animal by using their own pigment granules, iridophores are merely reflecting light back—*depending on the angle you're looking at the animal from.*

Now, you'd think that this would be enough for the cephalopod. It's already so much more than the rest of us have access to. Nope. It wonders, what about predators (or fleeing prey) that might still find me by my outline? That wouldn't do at all, would it?

Enter papillae.

Papillae are sections of the skin that can be deformed to make a texture bumpy. Even humans possess them (goosebumps) but cannot use them in the manner that cephalopods can. For instance, the use of these cells is how an octopus can wrap itself over a rock and appear jagged or how a squid or cuttlefish can imitate the look of a coral reef by growing miniature towers on its skin. It actually matches the texture of the substrate it chooses.

Finally, the leucophores: According to a paper, published in *Nature*,

> Cuttlefish and octopuses possess an additional type of reflector cell called a leucophore. They are cells that scatter full spectrum light so that they appear white in a similar way that a polar bear's fur appears white. Leucophores will also reflect any filtered light shown on them, for instance, they will reflect green light if green is presented to them.

Simply put, these help the animal blend into the background. If the water appears blue at a certain depth, the octopuses and cuttlefish can appear blue; if the water appears green, they appear green, and so on and so forth.

All these powers work together, or separately as needed, to create the most sophisticated camouflage known to us.

What is now such an obvious concept—using colour and light and shadow to hide—was not always so. In the 1980s, an American artist and nature enthusiast called Abbott Thayer put forth a then-radical idea: concealing colouration. He argued that colouration plays a role in protection and predation in nature, meaning animals actively use colour to navigate, attack and defend themselves.

The idea of camouflage was obviously around long before then; warriors used headdresses and warpaint long before Thayer cited them as examples of using disruptive camouflage. This means that strong, random patterns of colour flatten and break up outlines, rendering the person or animal or thing almost invisible. However, no one before him had put together this kind of documented research on the subject. He firmly believed that only an artist could have made these discoveries, considering their intense understanding of colour. He showed, through carefully made artwork, how 'the upper areas of animals tend to be darker than their shadowed undersides. Thus, the overall tone is equalised.' This renders the animal difficult to spot. It is possible that his research on disruptive patterns and countershading played a role in modern camouflage used in the military, in uniforms and ships. He was considered a genius, although some of his theories, which admittedly stretched too far, were also criticized, most notably by Theodore Roosevelt, who went on to serve as the twenty-sixth President of the United States. His son, Gerald Thayer, published a summary of his discoveries as a book called *Concealing Coloration in the Animal Kingdom*.

Humans have been obsessed with the idea of being invisible for decades. This brings me to the question I had asked you at the beginning of this chapter.

What Superpower Did You Pick?

Most of the people that took this test with me chose invisibility. We think of invisibility in different ways. In this digital age, there are millions of us online, screaming for attention and validation, invisible still in a vast sea of clamouring voices. We want to be seen, to be followed, to be heard constantly. And yet, it's one of our most primal desires to be able to vanish.

Paradoxically, being invisible allows us an advantage over others, or even helps to hide our insecurities. In the experiment I started out mentioning, people who chose invisibility were said to be embracing their shadow, a part of their impulses they kept hidden, and it would, at some point or the other, despite your noblest intentions, 'lead you down a dark path'. Even *The Invisible Man* (penned by H.G. Wells in 1897) ultimately lost his life in a frenzy of violence, and Kevin Bacon's apt portrayal of the perverse side of *The Hollow Man* made us all cringe. If you chose flight, you practically chose freedom for self. So, while it might seem like a noble choice, it is, ultimately, self-serving.

There are labs working on the cephalopod camouflage to make an invisibility cloak for humans. I don't know about you, but I know we have been passed over for these powers for a reason. Animals benefit from this in ways we don't need.

While the cephalopods actively use their bodies to change colour and shape, ghost crabs are called so because of their almost transparent, hence 'ghostly' appearance. Unlike other crabs that scatter when discovered, or hold up their claws and clap as a sign of aggression (like the clapping crab), the maroon rock crab hunkers down, tucks its limb under itself, and becomes still. It does what it thinks is a stellar impression of a rock. I never have the heart to tell it otherwise, and just quietly play along. To use Thayer's understanding, I am not looking at it from a predator's perspective, so it's unfair to say this isn't working for it. Some nudibranchs, or sea slugs, pretend to appear to like their surroundings, and certain flatworms use mimicry to appear like toxin-carrying slugs.

All of this happens in an area that was largely invisible to me, before I started observing it and could no longer look away. That is what the intertidal zone is: a secret forest.

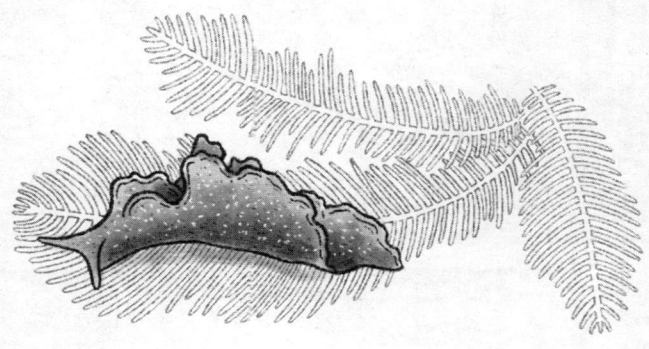

2

A SECRET FOREST

You are at the tideline.

Your feet are ensconced in the cool water swirling around your ankles.

Do you feel it?

In the distance, the sea meets the sky in a brilliant exchange of hues.

The horizon is preparing for the night.

Now, look around; the shallows are littered with rocks, pebbles and boulders.

You pick up a small rock. Now, under just one rock, you might find: a sea sponge (often mistaken for a plant but very much an animal), worms building tube homes, porcelain crabs scurrying for cover, sea slugs grazing on algae on the rock, sea stars moving slowly, sea snails laying eggs — I could go on.

Clockwise from top left: Meet the intertidal sprinters, the ghost crabs; breaking ingredients down for sandy beaches; look how they shine for you; sand art by the sand bubbler crabs

Look further into the distance. See, there's a murder of crows, egrets too, all waiting for their dinner. Look further still. There's a fishing boat docked, rocking back and forth gently as the water laps against the hull.

You pick up another rock with more animals, different permutations, varying combinations. And slowly you realize that under each rock is a secret forest. And under the sand, burrowing animals exist. Each of these mini-forests has a system — there are predators, there is prey and there are grazing meadows of algae.

Let's go closer.

Scientists believe that what you see on an intertidal zone is just one-third of what exists. The other bits are hidden. What if you cracked open this rock? Organisms like worms, clams and shrimps tunnel into the rocks and live inside them. Now, imagine thousands of rocks strewn over numerous coasts across the country, and around the globe. Can you imagine the scale of life sitting on our shores?

Look towards the land. In a terrestrial jungle, animals pick their territories, don't they? Tigers, bison, elephants, snakes, birds — they all pick parts of the forest that help them thrive.

That's what habitat means, doesn't it?

Rohit Majumdar, a professor at the School of Environment and Architecture, defines 'habitat' as something more than the physical dwelling. It is not just a structure, but an ecology of spaces that one inhabits every day. This means spaces beyond the building in which one stays, and it could also include surrounding spaces and other neighbouring regions. It's a place that is an intersection of what keeps us alive, in terms of food, safety and social circles.

As humans, we don't pick these spaces lightly, do we? We spend months, years, and even lifetimes to own that perfect space. Similarly, in the intertidal zones, marine creatures pick their spaces. Although it is an impermanent housing space, they do not pick at random.

Ghost crabs live in the upper intertidal regions, where water hardly ever reaches and they can hunt and scavenge. Sand bubbler crabs build condos in the sand to escape the water. Sea stars get a closer view of the ocean and live in the lower intertidal zones, where water rushes in first, so they don't have to do without it for longer than is necessary. Porcelain crabs prefer spaces under rocks, while nassarius snails burrow in the sand. Certain species of limpets (a kind of mollusc) have strong homing instincts and will come back 'home' after grazing. They have a broad foot that allows them to move across the rocks and also clamps down when they're stationary. They create mucus trails and are known to follow them back to their rocky homes. They pick rocks, which have slight indentations, which match the outline of their shells, and then rub their shells against the rock, grinding it until they fit perfectly, creating what is known as a 'home scar'.

The soldier crab is made for hard work in the intertidal zone. If you've gone to a sandy beach, and have seen circular rangoli-type sand patterns, you've been around these crabs. Like most crabs, it has elongated pincers that face each other to facilitate its meals. It gobbles up sand, sifts it for the thin coating of detritus (organic matter), and leaves behind the pellets in circular patterns resembling what could be described as crustacean art.

In terms of real estate, it's a bit of a hustler. Its home has two components — a vertical underground burrow that it lives in, and a temporary air chamber appropriately called an igloo.

Why? Well, a study found the need for a temporary structure. While building the igloo, the crab rotates like a corkscrew in wet sand, making circular walls and a roof out of sand pellets, resulting in an igloo that doubles as an air chamber. The crab can then burrow deeper down into the sand using this same action, away from the incoming tide and predators it may bring.

The lower intertidal zone is full of peril; when the tide returns, the shallows invite predators. The upper intertidal zone is no less difficult, where animals battle the harshest sun. Each animal finds its place, and knows its place. They understand the idea of home according to their needs, not anything else. In that, they probably navigate real estate better than us and have also evolved to live in harsh conditions.

Just like a terrestrial ecosystem, this is a giant wheel with cogs that fit together, with a legitimate food chain and web operating smoothly. Cut things out, and there'll be trouble, as an influential American researcher famously found out. In an experiment that put the science of ecology on a new course, Robert Paine chose two shores as his fields of study. On one, he started to remove sea stars (*Pisaster ochraceus*) from the lower intertidal zones in 1963. Over the next few years, he observed that in the absence of this predator, its prey, the mussel (*Mytilus californi*) expanded its territory and moved downward, overgrowing and overthrowing algae, barnacles and other creatures that preferred to live there. Soon, they declared mussel supremacy in the area.

We already know that an ecosystem is connected, but we don't usually see our shores as one. When a food chain is disrupted, everything goes off the rails. The heron that comes to feed, the egret that waits for its dinner, the crows that attempt to follow the fisher trail, the waders and the pipers — all species suffer from the disruption. This is all a space for convergence; it holds the ecological value of a forest, but just of a different kind than what we're used to.

And here's where the idea of a secret forest comes home.

What is a home, really? It provides safe spaces, food and connections. The animals live in habitats suited to them. The sand on a beach makes this habitat. Sandy beaches are made of these: broken rocks, silica, broken coral, fish poop, minerals, microorganisms called foraminifera and other things I won't ever know the names of.

But what I do know is this: these grains that seem so inconsequential individually, without weight or purpose, together form forces of nature for the creatures of the intertidal zones. They become homes. They're soft and yielding to ghost crabs and worms that need to burrow, shifting to accommodate as much space as they need. They're hard and thick for the sand bubblers, agreeing to be tossed and thrown and made pellets of. They provide an unwavering anchor against the waves to the eggs laid on the sand. Sand dune ecosystems stand guard at the coasts, even more effective against cyclones on the east coast of the country, which is prone to this interaction from the sea. Sand allows itself to be probed and pulled, just to be moulded by tiny hands that construct castles against the sea. If we could just learn when to be strong, and when to yield, or how to provide shelter, and how to be ready, when the time comes, to let go and scatter. If only we could learn how to be havens.

Homes do as is needed.

You look out again, where the sea meets the sky, and realize with a sudden certainty: all horizons might look the same, but every shore is different. It has to be. Because every shore is a home.

And it's alive.

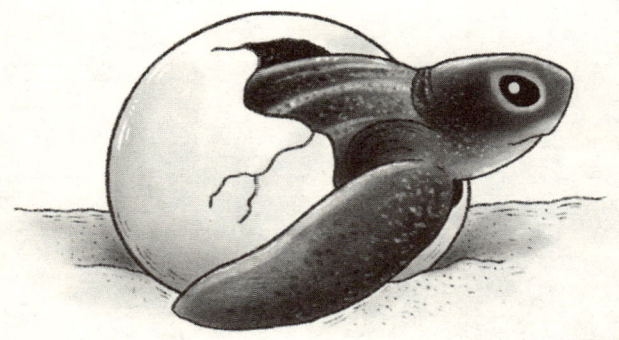

3

THE POWER OF CREATION

It looked just like bubble wrap.

Or, it looked like a white, soggy flower, coated in bubble wrap. There were a fair number of them across the beach: a foot long perhaps, fanned out, with five long 'petals', each jiggling with tiny bubble-like protrusions. They seemed to be anchored into the sand.

So many things on the beach can remind you of something else. In bigger cities, our trash is a tease. A blue tarp string will behave like a floating tentacle, or a transparent bag floating in the shallows will remind you of a jellyfish. Coming back to the bubble-wrapped flower, I could have dismissed it as a soggy plastic blob, but by then, I knew better. So, I looked closer.

Inside each bunch, lay a tiny nursery.

Each bubble held the tiniest squid baby you ever saw.

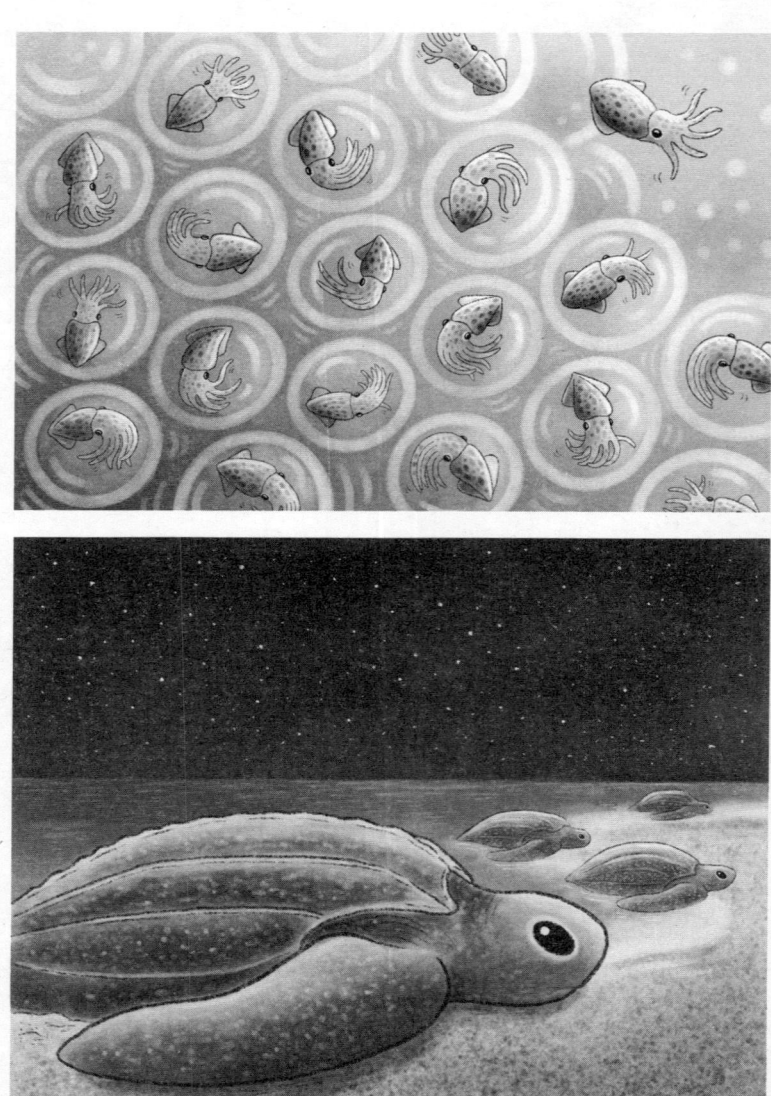

Our coasts are nurseries — squid babies raring to break free; leatherback turtles arriving to nest

Each bubble was an egg, and because the babies were now ready to hatch, I could see an oval body that flashed red and white, and . . . eyes. They were all part of the flower-like entity, which was an entire egg mass of hundreds of these.

I looked up and saw another egg mass in the distance, and another. There were heaps of them containing hundreds of babies in each at various stages of development. This was not the Juhu beach I knew. For now, squid mums had claimed it for a nursery — except that it was on one of the most popular beaches in Mumbai. It was an evening like any other: cricket was being played at every possible pitch length, romancing couples were ignoring a thousand pairs of prying eyes, people were walking, playing, exercising, eating — it was business as usual. Except it wasn't.

Alive.

That's the word we left off at in the previous chapter.

A place that facilitates creation.

The fact that there are babies here should come as no surprise. It *is* an ecosystem, the intertidal zone. Sea slugs, sea snails and other residents lay eggs here in small sacs; juvenile crabs are seen scampering across the shores, sea sponges grow up here. But this was interesting because squids are not intertidal residents. They live in the ocean. A number of open ocean creatures come to the shores to lay eggs: turtles, octopuses, and cuttlefish to name a few. Fish species come to the shallows to lay their eggs. A walk along the intertidal region will reveal juveniles of damselfish, angelfish and puffers all zipping along, learning the ropes before their journey to the deep.

Even horseshoe crabs come to the shore every year now, guided by the full moon, to lay their eggs in spite of the increasing danger to their lives — they're traded for their medicinal properties. Turtles use the dry areas of the shore, the area just above the tideline — it is not strictly the intertidal zone, but just the part that never gets wet. It's natural for animals to choose spaces that would ensure the safety of their babies, and there are fewer predators in this zone, compared to in their homes. Not that the intertidal region is entirely safe — other terrestrial creatures, birds and even humans might, more often than not, get at and harm the juveniles.

Although sea turtles aren't strictly intertidal creatures, their relationship with this stretch of land is primal and intense. I am stretching this narrative to beyond the tideline, so not technically the intertidal region, but just beyond, further up the shore. They land here to give birth and choose the sand for temperature-based gender selection of their babies. After the young ones hatch, they take their first steps across the shore into the comforting embrace of the ocean, which they recognize instinctively with no help, as the place that their mums came from.

The Long Walk to Freedom and Back

Hermit Crab watches as the humans run about on the beach.
They are carrying notes, call sheets, making teams, being
        generally chaotic.
They are being extremely human, she decides.
All this stress and anxiety hovering in the air.
Ruining, thinks Hermit Crab, the exciting energy actually
        running through the sand,
Blowing in the breeze, making the atmosphere thick with
        anticipation.
She looks towards the ocean.
They are almost here.
Hermit Crab staggers away slowly to a vantage point.
She likes watching this annual homecoming.

She even grudgingly likes the name humans had kept for it.
The Spanish word, arribada. 'Arrival', by sea.
She watches the humans with flashlights, sharing a laugh with
*   the fishers who've come to watch. She likes that the fishers*
*   knew more than the scientists who visit.*
And she likes that the scientists understand that.
You and I, my man, she calls out to a passing local who doesn't
*   hear her.*
She doesn't mind. He knows she is here.
We know this place. We are familiars, she thinks, comfortably
*   settling in.*
She wonders how many would come.
And then, as the moon lights up the waves, they arrive.
Olive ridley turtles. Riding the waves to the shore.
A hundred turtles riding each wave, can you even imagine that?
Suddenly, everything is electric.
Over the next five days, the ladies arrive in thousands,
Gorgeous surfers breaking surface and riding to the coast to lay
*   eggs.*
Hermit Crab and her friends wave them in, and celebrate.
The humans cheer, and get to work, counting thousands of nests
*   to record.*
Can you imagine this kind of turn in the ocean?
Like a frequency only women catch.
Yes, yes she knows there's the earth's magnetic field at play here.
But, whatever it is, for that week,
Every night is ladies' night.

~

Every year, on a beach in Odisha, a spectacular event occurs.

Around the same time, every year, the fishers would know that the arrival was imminent. And sure enough, over the next few nights, tens of thousands of turtles, as if by some unspoken agreement, would ride over the waves to lay their eggs on this shore. Arribada.

Muralidharan Manoharakrishnan has been working with fisher communities and collecting data on turtles for the last twelve years. 'The fishermen know everything, even the regions the turtles preferred', he said. He added:

Their knowledge is based on experience; it is generational. Just like they know where to fish for what, when prawns will be bountiful, when is a good time to catch sardines. How they look at moon phases, tides and then they could predict, that turtles will come. Working closely with them while collecting turtle data was a huge learning for an urban minded scientist like me.

By the time Murali saw his first nesting in 2009, he had read almost every piece of literature available on the phenomenon. It was also part of his master's dissertation, so he knew it would be an important data point. He thought he knew exactly what was going to happen.

But when they arrived, he was mesmerized: 'I had walked on that stretch of beach many times by then. A 5-kilometre stretch where usually everything is quiet and absolutely normal. And then one night, I am watching thousands of turtles riding each wave towards the shore.'

Read that again. Thousands of turtles riding each wave. He recalls: 'It's an unforgettable experience. It's like nothing you'll ever see; the photos you've seen, the videos you think have prepared you is all just detail. Nothing prepares you for this consistent arrival over five nights.'

The turtles come incessantly, avalanching the shore, with their precious cargo. Murali and the others are on nest duty and have to patrol the beach every hour to count the new nests and read the numbers and head out again. 'It's tough labour. A usual workday is from 6 p.m. to 6 a.m. You end up wishing by the third night that more don't come,' he laughs. Olive ridley turtles nest on many parts of our shores. Of course, this beach is one of the largest congregations — by quite a margin compared to any other part of the Indian coastline. The villagers and the fishers come with their kids to watch. 'It's a celebratory event here', says Murali, and adds that 'under no circumstances would I want this to change into a closed, elite group of people. Everyone should experience this'.

On a dark night in 2020, marine biologist Naveen Namboothri was walking along the shores of Galathea Bay on the Great Nicobar Island. The island beaches are an experience, and not just because of the picturesque shoreline, but also because of what lives there. The beaches are fine sand, the littoral forest canopies are close to the water's edge and the intertidal zones are bursting with life. A scientist interested in lesser-known creatures even as a student, Naveen studied at the Centre for Advanced Studies in Marine Biology, Annamalai University, a remote marine research station in Parangipettai that he remembers laid the foundation for a remarkable curiosity and understanding of the marine realm.

Naveen was on a research project with twelve other people, who were working on different parts of life on the shore. Naveen has worked in the marine realm for more than twenty years now and has navigated different shores across the country. At Galathea, he was looking for invertebrates, a study of wildlife close to his heart, preferring to work on lesser-known creatures than the charismatic ones, which already have a fair bit of help. 'Everything about the islands is fascinating', he says of his invaluable experiences while working in Nicobar. He adds:

> The forests are unlike any others; the interiors are remote with mind-boggling diversity. But what also makes it interesting is the human footprint here. If you walk along the intertidal for a 100 m, you'll probably find waste originating from 25–30 countries, possibly due to its proximity to the Strait of Malacca, which is a busy shipping route.

On that night, an excited group of researchers working on sea turtles invited him to watch the nesting process. 'I'll be honest', he said laughing, as he recalled that night that 'for marine biologists like me, turtles are like terrestrial animals almost, and there are only seven species, and I always wondered at the hue and cry about these seven species'. They resignedly switched off their lights to keep the beaches dark and comfortable for the turtles and sat under the clear sky to watch.

In less than an hour, a leatherback sea turtle emerged from the ocean, making its way to the beach. Now, compared to other sea turtles, an adult leatherback is a giant. On a dark beach, they saw a 5 to 6 feet reptile crawl out of the water to lay her eggs on the shore.

'There was bioluminescent plankton in the water that night', said Naveen, caught up in the memory. He continued:

> Can you imagine it? The turtle slowly moving across the beach, illuminated against the dark background, and the dark, dark sky with almost no haze. The stars were all out and shining; it was like sitting in a planetarium. The beach seems such a powerful

life-giving space, and you get to watch the powers in play. You can hear the turtle moving up the slope of the beach, you hear it heave, you can hear the flippers thud against the sand as it lumbers its way up. You see it throwing sand around, an almost dramatic sight as it starts to dig at a spot. It starts laying eggs slightly bigger than a table tennis ball and towards the end you can see these tiny unfertilised eggs, some smaller than your finger nail. It's so surreal. This colossal creature that can elegantly [be] swimming across the oceans, yet be so cumbersome on the beach, laying these eggs, and then camouflaging the nest, before she's gone for good.

He remembers being transfixed at that time, three hours later, and even years after the experience.

As I write this chapter, news is coming in of construction at Galathea Bay. The leatherbacks returned after the effects of the tsunami in 2004 rocked the islands, and now this new port will be another perplexing addition to their travels. I hope that the resilience that we so easily tether to all living things doesn't become something we start to take for granted.

Years ago in Chambal, far inland from the coast, I was lucky enough to watch hatchlings of the critically endangered red-crowned roofed turtle (*Batagur kachuga*) crawl/walk/waddle into a river—not a marine ecosystem, but a freshwater one. It was a heartening experience. On its way to the river, one of the babies made a pit stop on my foot. I stood as still as a rock while it rested on my big toe, afraid to even breathe so as to not scare it, every dormant maternal instinct bubbling in concern for this child. The lead researcher came over smiling and said, completely clinically, 'Only 2 per cent survival rate. Most will perish from predators.' I looked at him incredulously, but he stomped on, oblivious, 'That's why they give birth in these large numbers. Birds, canids, fish, everything eats eggs and babies.' I started to laugh; some scientists cannot read a room at all. Oh, put your pitchforks down, people. I said 'some'.

Coming back to the coast, this land at the edge of the sea is essential to breeding, and sometimes yields delightful sights of juvenile creatures that you would otherwise need to dive underwater for—like pufferfish, damselfish, sting rays or guitarfish—whether it's a rocky, sandy or mangrove intertidal region.

That day at Juhu beach, a few of us were huddled around a squid egg sac that was almost ready to hatch. We waited on our haunches, careful to allow the babies some room, just like one would do in a maternity ward, where babies are put in little beds with a window through which you can see them. That was us, the doting neighbourhood that had come to gush over the newborns.

The winter months allowed many interactions with infants. While the squid prefers to anchor her eggs on the sand, cuttlefish use secure, solid objects like rocks, sea fans (a kind of tree-shaped soft coral) or the anchor ropes of nearshore fishing boats. From a distance, cuttlefish eggs look like little black grapes. But just like squid eggs, go closer, and if they're ready to hatch, you'll see little cuttlefish somersaulting inside each sac, complete with beating mantles, tentacles and camouflage tools, pulsating red spots that travel along their bodies like dots on a map. You'll also notice big eyes staring up and out, wondering what lies beyond, what awaits them, whether it's danger or delight.

I reckon if we could hear them, there'd be a fair bit of screaming and yelling. Some were zipping inside, absolutely eager to come out into the world (yes, who's going to tell them?), while others napped, floating dreamily in their small, literal bubbles.

If you're wondering how the babies survive without their mums, who leave almost immediately afterwards, don't worry, readers — she thought of everything. Each offspring has a yolk sac in front of its face that feeds and nourishes it. It makes the babies look exactly like miniature proboscis monkeys or clown noses. This sac will shrink as the baby gets bigger, disappearing once it's ready to hatch.

This was the case for most of the squid offspring that we observed. Our group watched, completely hooked by the sight as they began to emerge. It was all very Jurassic Park-esque, where scientists and naturalists gathered around a dinosaur emerging from its egg. As they started to emerge, I could see their smooth, glistening skins, shining with new life, and oh dear lord, the chromatophores! In front of our stunned eyes, we saw these patterns appear and disappear like flashing red spots on the white surfaces, preparing for a life with superpowers.

The shore offers a strange cycle of life and death. Some of the largest creatures of the deep are washed ashore, stranded or deposited after death. Sometimes, shells of ancient creatures are washed ashore. On a field trip to Ariyalur, Tamil Nadu, Suvrat Kher, a geologist, found fossils of ammonites, which are extinct cephalopods! He found that the area was underlain by Cretaceous age fossil-rich sedimentary rocks that were deposited in rivers, coastal settings (like beaches) and in shallow intertidal and subtidal spaces. *The rocks are about seventy to eighty million years old.* 'Such a variety of depositional settings means a variety of organisms living in them', says Suvrat. He adds, 'You can see plant leaf impressions, many types of molluscs (including ammonoids), coral fragments and even tinier organisms like foraminifera and calcareous nanoplankton, which are seen only under a microscope. An ancient long vanished world comes to life.'

In so many ways, it offers us a glimpse into what lies underneath the surface. It might not tell us exactly how they died and what happened to them. But you have proof that they lived. And with the new babies, you have proof that they will.

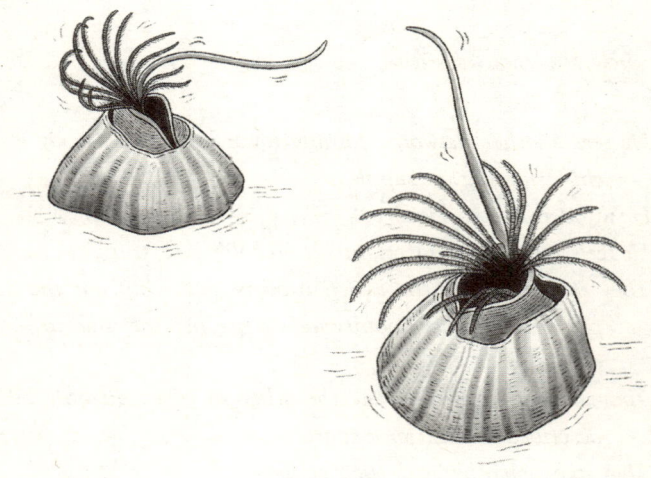

LET'S TALK ABOUT SEX, BABY

The sun is setting on the beaches of Goa.

In a few hours, the shacks and restaurants will switch their psychedelic lights on, put on a thumping beat and Goa will ready itself for a night out on the town.

Even on the shore, the party is well under way.

Hermit Crab is busy tending to her tide pool, the usual venue for weekend shenanigans.

Her friends, the sea snails were passing around algae for appetizers.

A flatworm walks in, ignores the others, checks his reflection in the tide pool.

Satisfied, he looks around. He wonders what his partner has worn.

*He sees another flatworm coming towards him. His body is
    thin, rippling and supple.*
He wonders how this will go.
He feels a thrill. The uncertainty is probably everything.
*They take position, the two flatworms, and whip out their
    penises — which are pointy and sharp. Then they start to . . .
    duel.*
*They attempt to impregnate the other in what can only be
    described as an extreme sport.*
*They stab each other with their penises,
    hoping to be the first one to get their sperm in the other.*
*Hermaphrodites, they have both male and female organs, but
    they both want to avoid carrying the babies due to the
    energy and time commitment.*
*So, they fight with each other to ensure they are the impregnator
    not the impregnated.*
Hermit Crab rolls her eyes. So typical.

~

If you think this bit is bizarre, the reproductive devices in the
intertidal zones will really capture your imagination. The eggs
that you read about in the last chapter, where did they all come
from?

While humans share the concept of perpetuation and survival
of our species, we have fewer means to do this. Over the years, I
have seen loads of shore species getting it on, and now that I've
said this, I would not be surprised if I were among a watch list of
perverts made by the shore sheriff. While the human race might
gloat about inventing the *Kama Sutra*, I have to tell you, we can't
hold a candle to shore life.

Myths around the beginning of the human race are abundant and some of it includes coastal life. In *Spirals in Time*, Dr Scales notes:

> In the Pacific Northwest of North America, the Haida people believe their creator, the trickster Raven, dug up a cockleshell after a flood and opened it to release the men inside. Raven then persuaded the men to have sex with another mollusc, the chiton and the resulting offspring were women.

What an astounding visual, this. The chiton is an oval-shaped mollusc, and looks like it's wearing eight-plated armour through the length of its body. Maybe it was the uniform, do you think?

The overachievers that they are, they have different ways of making an art form out of romance: sexual and asexual. Okay, that's simple.

Sexual reproduction involves the obvious existence of an egg and a sperm. This is, of course, through good old-fashioned sexual intercourse, or external reproduction also known as spawning. Basically, the animals will release eggs and sperm into the water and they fertilize outside the body, and voila, become larvae. Humans have some versions of both of these, as you know.

Asexual reproduction is the other rather enviable route available for these creatures:

There's budding—it's like a bump that grows on the surface of the animal and slowly becomes a separate creature. Then there's fission, where the animal clones itself into two. Finally, there's fragmentation, where if it happens to break away from the main creature, the broken segment grows into a new animal. Although, relying on just asexual reproduction could limit genetic variation, and there would also be limited dispersal of the animal.

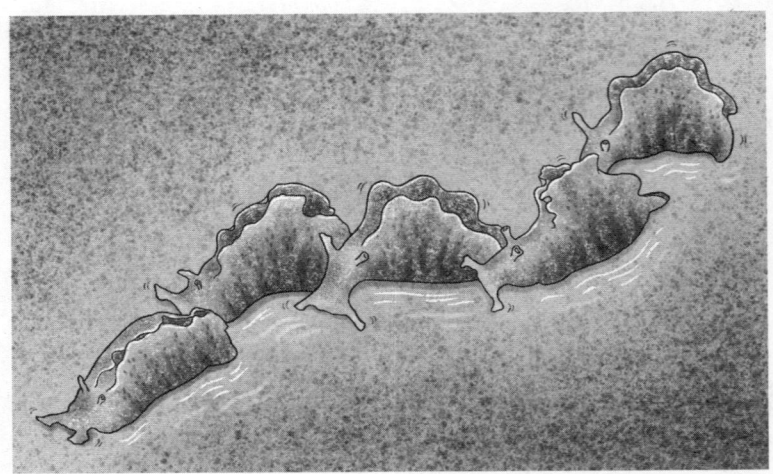

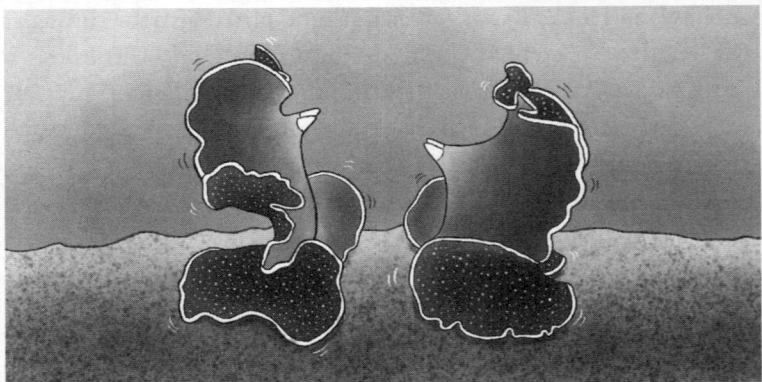

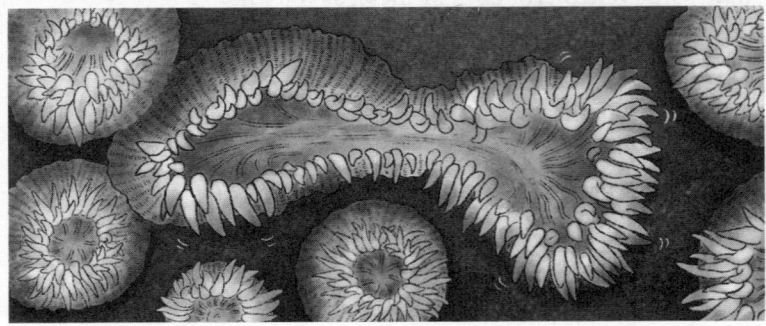

From top: The weird sexy tales of the coasts — a regular sea hare orgy; penis duelling with the flatworms and fission aka cloning with a sea anemone

The path to these two reproductive possibilities is lined with some strange sex stories. So, get your cuppa, and let's go.

Superpower Category: Strange Sex

Meet the flatworm. Never has a name sat so well for a creature. Thin as a flattened ribbon and fluid as lava, it slides over rocky patches with liquid grace. It seems to pour rather than move over things, due to the constantly beating 'cilia' (minute hair-like structures that help in movement) that carry its flat body over surfaces. Many also swim by rolling the sides of their bodies like waves.

Polyclad (meaning 'many branches') flatworms earn their name from their highly branched intestine that quickly carries nutrients to the furthest reaches of the body. This makes complete sense; I really don't know where it'd put the food with such a strangely shaped body that lacks any blood. And because literally nothing else might probably fit in there, it needs to digest its food outside its body. The digestive juices that it injects help liquefy the prey outside the body, and then the flatworm sucks the pulp in.

Those are just a few things about these other-worldly creatures. Some species of flatworms have this strange way of making sure their legacy is forwarded to the future. They have both male and female organs as they are hermaphrodites, but they will fight with each other to be the impregnator; being impregnated means bearing the burden of carrying babies, which requires energy and the commitment of time and other resources.

They fence with their penises to decide this battle's end. They will try and stab the other worm anywhere on the body with their penis to pass the sperms into the body. Marine researcher Sudhanshu Dixit has watched this phenomenon, called hypodermic impregnation, unfold in his lab.

Queue Up for This Orgy, Please

In hermaphrodite creatures, sometimes there's an understanding of sorts. Some species of flatworms do, in fact, exchange sperm and don't go to town with the slasher stabbing. The sea hare's mating congregation is an example of a mutually beneficial, well-planned orgy.

At first glance, the sea hare, from the superfamily Aplysioidea, is a perplexing creature.

Imagine a really rotund slug. Done? Now give it two tentacles on its head. Now give it two more antennae-type protrusions — rhinophores, which it uses to sense dissolved molecules in the water. Other sea slugs have these as well, but when married with this creature's bulk, they make it look like a hare. Now add parapodia — fleshy flaps that unfurl from the sides of the body when they move across tide pools. Now, what you have is an animal that looks like a cross between a sea slug and a rabbit wearing a poncho, in the middle of a transfiguration spell from Harry Potter's book of spells gone awry. And here comes the kicker: its penis is on the side of its head.

On a research trip, Vishal Bhave, a marine biologist based out of Ratnagiri, was documenting the presence of sea slugs at low tide and came across an oddly long line of sea hares. He was surprised to see the animals queued up, against each other. This is sometimes how these creatures mate.

Sea hares don't always mate in aggregations, but it is seen to happen often enough. Researchers have seen any number between two to even thirty at a time. Various factors could induce this — the season, salinity, food plants, temperatures, and so on. While each hare has both male and female reproductive organs, they need a mate to reproduce — they cannot simply use both sets of organs on their own. Size does matter here, though. The sea hares playing the sperm givers look for mates which are larger in size, indicating a potential for larger clutches of eggs. They mate in a line, where the one inserts its penis (located at the front of the body) into the vagina (located at the rear) of the other sea hare. They're not in any rush about this entire process. Mating aggregations have been known to last hours, days, or even weeks.

So they know the role playing script beforehand and everyone ends up satisfied (I don't know what happens to the first and the last sea hares). I do feel that a circle might be more effective, but I am not the director of this orgy, so I am guessing they know best.

Gender Fluidity Is a Superpower

Marah J. Hardt's laugh riot, *Sex in the Sea*, explores the various ways in which marine life reproduce in a deliciously irreverent style. The subjects do inspire irreverence of a kind. There are many forms of hermaphroditism: sequential and simultaneous are two main strategies. Simultaneous hermaphroditism is when the same individual has both male and female sex organs, whereas sequential hermaphroditism allows the creature to switch genders.

Clownfish have a pecking order where mating is concerned, and it's naturally to do with size. The largest female (because she can carry more eggs) mates with the largest male, and they lord it over the rest of the clan. The female has all the power — she ensures that the male is big enough, but also that it doesn't grow too big to then convert into the female and upset the sperm cart. The male, on the other hand, keeps all the other males in check, traumatizing them to a place of, as Hardt calls it, 'pre-pubescent limbo' so they don't steal the female. After the female dies, the male turns into a female queen, so to speak, and the next male steps up to mate with her. Are you seeing where I am going with this? In *Finding Nemo*, after his mum died, his dad would have ideally turned into a female clownfish and mated with Nemo! I can see your kids' eyes tearing up, so I'm sorry, go take a water break.

There are many species of fish which have both male and female organs, and can (and do) change their gender based on the best way to make babies. Wrasses do the opposite. A male is the king of his harem, sure, but if he dies, or even leaves for a longish period of time, a dominant female will turn into the male and take over his harem to mate. The concept of a big female is the default in nature, because it has better egg-bearing capacity. In wrasses, it is reversed because there is 'sexual selection' based on machismo and colour, and the advantage of being big and macho has overtaken (evolutionarily) the advantage of a big, female body. Understandable — and here we think our dating pool is tough.

Care Package from the Cephalopods

Some of the over achieving cephalopods accomplish egg transfer in a novel way. 'There's no clear genetic study done on this', Aditi Pophale says, and adds a disclaimer:

> This is what the natural history studies say: The third arm on the male is the penis arm (called the hectocotylus). It has a sperm

packet, which it transports to the female, who doesn't need to fertilise the eggs right away. She can store multiple packets from multiple males. And here's where it gets a bit complex because of the lack of genetic studies, but she either uses one sperm packet to fertilise all her eggs, or gambles and chooses different packets for some of her eggs and so on. The male has no say and no idea if she will in fact end up choosing his sperm.

I particularly like the cephalopod saga because the female has so much choice in the matter, because males don't know whose sperm she's going to choose. Certain species of squid and cuttlefish also do this. In the octopus's case, after this point, it's an all-female plot; she does not need the male anymore. In fact, there have been reports of the female cannibalizing the male after laying her eggs.

This is probably because egg-laying is an energy-consuming exercise for her. She lays, and then continuously protects and oxygenates the eggs. She doesn't leave her den during this time, even to feed. So she's preparing for almost a month of fasting afterwards. That's hard work; the eggs are the size of grapes, so sometimes, algae could grow on them or something could come eat them. She needs to constantly tend to them, clean them and save them. After she releases them, she dies. But the males won't ever attack the female; she has all the genetic material. They'll probably fight other males and compete, even in the midst of an active mating situation.

Reproduction is the male's siren song as well, in some ways. After mating a couple of times, they stop hunting, changing colour, even their skin begins to lose lustre and sometimes even develops lesions. In literature, they call it senescence. They start behaving erratically. If we were to put a human emotion to it, it would resemble senility. They live life in the fast lane — they grow fast, live fast, and die fast. Of course, this is also species specific. Bigger octopuses could live longer, and regions and water temperature also decide how they long they live. But the step to mate, for the cephalopod, is literally one step closer to death.

Superpower Category: Clones R Us

Imagine a world where creating new life is as simple as that for an anemone.

Meet the charismatic sea anemone which, in a show of self-reliance, can split into two *and become two separate individuals*. The sea anemone stretches along its base and literally splits along the middle — this is called longitudinal fission.

The other way is called pedal laceration. Here many small tissue fragments come away from the oral (pedal) disc and become new anemones. Although the idea of reproduction through fission is attractive, what a strange world that would be. People just splitting into versions of themselves. No super-technology needed to literally clone ourselves into versions and live out our multiple lives. The very thought of it makes my brain hurt. We'd all cheat and use this in so many terrifying ways. It's really no surprise that humans got just the powers they needed.

There are many creatures in the intertidal zone that have this ability — sea sponges, corals, brittle stars, and a good many others. The sea anemone is a magical sight on a shore. Named after the terrestrial plant, it looks more like a flower than an animal. Do you remember its deep-sea cousins from *Finding Nemo*? Those colourful, swaying tentacles made for some prime real estate for Nemo and his ocean-traversing daddy, didn't they?

I am yet to meet a group of people who haven't been gobsmacked by this animal when they come tidepooling to the shore. Different species wear colourful outfits, translucent tentacles that ripple, expand and contract with the tide. On a sandy beach, you'll see the pearly sea anemone (*Paracondylactis sinensis*) with fleshy pink tentacles tipped with stinging cells luxuriously spread out on the brown sand, appearing to bloom as it extends its tentacles to feed while the tide rolls in. The tentacles are attached to an oral disc in the centre, which is like a mouth, so to speak. On a rocky shore, the column of the green striped anemone (*Diadumene lineata*), with which it attaches itself on a rock, will remind you strongly of Obelix's (of *Asterix and Obelix* fame) pants, or the blood moon appearance of the burgundy anemone.

Something Green, Something Borrowed and Something Blue

Another animal that uses fission is the zoantharian. Zoantharians are a type of cnidarian and they have stinging cells (their cousins include jellyfish, hydroids, coral, anemones, etc.). Just like the anemone, they split along their length into two. These animals have won hearts all over the world because of how they look. Let me paint you a picture.

In Malvan, Maharashtra, when I stepped on the shore locally known as 'Rock Garden', I could hardly see the rock surface underneath. The entire lower intertidal zone was covered with tightly packed colonies of zoantharians. It looked like a giant honeycomb. I had to be careful and step on patches that didn't have the animals living on them. And these animals are closed when the tide is out, so they look like tightly packed blobs. They look like miniature anemones, but closed.

I was reminded of the movies of the 1990s about outer space that had squishy, springy blobs as aliens. Surely this is another dimension, I thought, as I bent down for a closer look. The rocks were covered with life, with no room to spare at all. They sat with their tentacles closed over their faces.

But then the tide flowed in at this Rock Garden. Seawater poured into the tide pools and over the zoantharians, and they started to open. Their tentacles spread out like the sun. And you see what they had been hiding within, as if they were trying to dim their beauty for some part of the day to provide a semblance of self-esteem to the animals around them. The oral disc is fluorescent blue and green in colour. I looked around as the polyps opened up — it was like meeting hundreds of peacock feathers, glowing in the water. What was this sorcery?

Here's some folklore for you. Known as 'Limu-make-o-Hana' (seaweed of death from Hana) on the Hawaiian island of Maui, *Palythoa* zoanthids were believed to be born from the ashes of an evil 'Shark God' that the villagers had killed. Islanders traditionally smeared this creature on their spears. *Palythoa* zoanthids produce palytoxin, the second deadliest poison in nature. It remains to be seen whether the ones found in India are as toxic, but it's interesting to know that the toxin comes to the animal externally. It's hiring a potions master to do its job for it.

Zoantharians outsource things a fair bit. It is in a symbiotic relationship with zooxanthellae algae, which are dinoflagellates (a type of marine plankton). It takes the zooxanthellae from the surrounding seawater: the zooxanthellae uses photosynthesis to create food, and the surplus goes to the zoantharian. In turn, the algae get a space to call home.

Superpower Category: Spawn Central

I want you to imagine this: think of a sloping cliffside, the kind you've seen in Ireland tourism brochures. Can you see the Cliffs of Moher in your mind's eye — the cliff edge, the drop and the ocean below? If I've inadvertently taken you to the pages of *Rebecca*, that's pretty much the ambience I'm trying to recreate.

All along the cliff's side, imagine tiny, branched grass growing all the way to the bottom into the water, and until the seabed.

Do you see it?

Now imagine this in a miniature model, a foot-deep tide pool with hydroids as the branched grass. Hydroids are cnidarians, with stinging cells inside their polyps. There are many different species of hydroids, but this one is pinkish and white, with small polyps on the branches of a fern-shaped colony (*Pennaria* — the Christmas tree hydroid) The name is important, because as it is in the frustrating world of science, not all species do one thing. So not all hydroids spawn like this.

Now it gets a bit wild.

These polyps, like tiny, tentacled suns, each have a mouth and gut.

The stem and branches you see is a network, a set of pipelines that deliver food to the entire colony, ensuring that the food collected by the polyps is distributed to all that need it. Communities that make our hearts sing.

We peered closer. We were already on our hands and knees, so it took considerable effort to not topple into the tide pool and create a tsunami for its inhabitants. I put my phone as close to the animal as I could without dipping it into the water — an unfortunately frequent accident in the intertidal zones — and activated the zoom function in the camera.

Small white particles, the size of dots, were surrounding the hydroids. Under the light of the torch, it looked like it was snowing in the tide pool, a little like the small particles of dust lit up by a beam of sunlight streaming into a room.

But in a second, some of the 'particles' did a purposeful jig.

Then there was another, an unmistakable, pulsating, rhythmic movement.

I gasped. 'Are those . . . is that . . .'

'Yes. Medusae,' whispered Abhishek.

The hydroid was releasing hydromedusae, whose purpose is to immediately reproduce and die. These look a bit like jellies, being from the same group. These little beings were pulsating dreamily in the pool.

These medusae, replete with gonads, will release sperms and eggs into the water, and these will form larvae that will swim to and colonize new rock surfaces as hydroid colonies. Essentially, this is the hydroid's brief stage for sexual reproduction, in a life of otherwise asexual budding.

Some coral species are broadcast spawners — they release eggs and sperms into the water and the reproduction happens in that manner. Then there are also brooders, which release ready larvae into the water. These colonies are expansive in the sea, and the intertidal zone of course has smaller and fewer ones in general. In coral and sea sponge colonies, the polyps can 'bud' off and spread the colony, a process aptly called 'budding'. They can even start new colonies from a broken fragment, in the right conditions — researchers have attempted to restore damaged reefs using this. But this sort of reproduction is more to extend and proliferate coral colonies, not to create new ones. Just like in a forest, it's beneficial

Forests under the surface. Hydroids releasing medusae into the tide pool

when the dispersal of seeds of trees, for example, happens far and wide and not just next door. It's also good when genes mix from time to time.

Superpower Category: Conquests and Takeovers

Harshal Karve, a marine biologist with Mangrove Foundation, Mumbai, is studying corals in the city's intertidal zone. The idea of corals turned on its head for him when he saw them on the shore at Poshitra in Gujarat. At the time, he was doing a study on sea snails for the Bombay Natural History Society. We think of corals as wildly colourful, expansive forests in the sea, hosting and sustaining a plethora of life. We think of corals as being somewhere far away—pristine beaches of white coral sand. We don't think of them as beings that are right on our shores.

On some shores in Gujarat, the tide rolls back kilometres into the distance, opening up a vast area of the intertidal zone. A usually stoic Karve, recalling the memory, lights up and says, 'The Gujarat intertidal was magic.' He adds:

> Brittle stars, sea stars, slugs, everything you've read about is out and about in full sight. We were planning a transect survey for gastropods (snails and slugs) in Narara Marine National Park, and Dwarka and I was already incredulous at seeing coral right up at the shore. But the next evening, I saw Poshitra and nothing could have prepared me for it.

When Harshal stepped onto the Poshitra intertidal zone, the sun had already dipped below the horizon. 'I was still new to tidepooling. I didn't even know I needed to carry a torch for evening tides,' he said. I understand this. Over the last four years, my wardrobe has grown to accommodate 'quick-dry' shore clothes, closed-toed waterproof shoes and a powerful torch to protect me from falling face down on sharp barnacles during an evening tide. Being unprepared in this zone can be extremely uncomfortable.

Harshal floundered around in the dark for a bit, trying to keep from slipping, when the senior researcher he was with asked him to switch on his phone's flashlight. He said, 'I thought the suggestion was to keep me from falling, but when I switched it on, I stopped in my tracks.' His eyes lit up at the memory: 'I was standing on a packed, literal carpet of corals. A glorious two-to-three-kilometre patch, as far as the light could see, right there, on the shore. I was stunned.'

Take a moment to understand this. All our interactions with coral have been through deep-sea documentaries. What are our immediate associations? The Great Barrier Reef, diving in the Andaman and Nicobar Islands, and Maldives vacations with diver tanks. When you see that this zone, this strange space that we largely think of as land, has representatives from their deep-sea counterparts, it is a special experience.

Imagine standing in the water with thousands of these colonies of different types of coral (numerous species of hard and soft coral) around you. So many animals, all packed together in gorgeous symmetry, like a housing society, but so much prettier.

And it's not just the animals that behave so outrageously. The winter months that run in on the heels of the monsoon bring with it the short-lived explosion of sea lettuce. On the shores of Goa, after the monsoon, Abhishek said of a bloom of *Enteromorpha* (now called *Ulva*), 'This seaweed proceeded to carpet entire stretches of rocky seashore in a vibrant green that seems almost gaudy.' He added:

> It is a short-lived period of bounty, but while the party lasts, all kinds of seashore herbivores flock here. The sunshine that dramatically triggers this awesome event is also the thing that, equally dramatically, draws the curtains on it. At the end of this bonanza (about a week or two at most), the sun beats down harshly enough to dry and bake the seaweed mat into a wafer-like crunchy film on the rock, almost metallic to look at.

It's things like this that I find other-worldly. On many occasions, I've felt that the intertidal zone is almost a parallel universe to the one we usually inhabit. It is something so removed from what I know and am familiar with, but right in plain sight. More than one tidepooler will tell you that it's like walking through a portal, onto the shore where these strange animals live and where nothing makes sense until you switch your mindset to the idea that now you're a guest and that this is a twilight zone.

~

Hermit Crab had a busy day
She had made a special food preparation for the new tide pool
> *tenant.*
She balanced the tray on her new shell — a bulky Babylonian
> *snail had just passed on,*
And she'd chanced upon her new home, God bless his soul.
Just a small gesture to welcome it to the neighbourhood.
It's a strange one, Nassa Mud Snail had told her yesterday over
> *their backyard chat.*
'It doesn't seem to have a face', she'd said.
She reached the rock the new tenant had arrived on.
There was a small hillock there, she noticed, with the top
> *flattened out.*
Like a volcano. Yes, one that had a slit that was shut for now.
A barnacle, she realized. That's what this was.
Barnacle larvae travel the ocean, looking for a home.
And when they find a place they like, these babies buy into it
> *for life.*
This one had settled in her neighbourhood.
Aw, she thought, giggling. A house-hunting baby.
She knocked on the side of the hillock.
Nothing. Not even the tiniest movement.

She called out, 'Hello! A welcome treat for you.'
After a second, the slit opened, and a pair of legs came out, took
the food away, dove back in and shut the flap right back.
Hermit Crab blinked at the silent volcano-ish structure.
A creature, encased face first inside a hard covering that it builds
for itself, feeding with its legs!
Billions of blistering barnacles, she thought, wryly. It is a strange one.

A few years ago, *Boss Baby*, a show that would have never entered my radar had it not been for my nieces, became the central conversation point at home. It is based on an animated movie about babies running offices, strategizing, making money and getting houses. It is set in a strange paradoxical universe where babies wear suits and make life decisions.

I was reminded of this strange programme when I learnt that the larvae of certain sessile species in the intertidal zone travelled around in the ocean, looking for a place to call home. For life.

Tiny offspring shopping for homes.

For this section, we'll look at some species which not only look for long-term real estate, but also have the understanding that if conditions remain favourable, they will colonize the shore, like a conquest — for example, corals, bryozoans, barnacles and oysters.

Let us count the ways.

All three species are able to reproduce sexually. They are all hermaphrodites, so the polyps release their sperm and ova into the water current, ultimately forming the house-hunting, free-swimming larvae. Now, this infant needs to find a suitable hard substrate, where it can settle to grow and form a colony.

Captain Haddock's Billions of Blistering Barnacles*

The barnacle is a strange concept. I was reminded of bats when I first got to know about it because the animal is upside down inside. You'll first meet a barnacle sitting alongside oysters on a rocky shore — many of them, actually. They're largely invasive creatures. The most common ones on our shores are the purple acorn barnacles. You'll find them on most hard surfaces — from rocks to shells to the hulls of ships, mangrove roots, floating jars, pillars of jetties, and so on. Captain Haddock hated them with good reason — they have been known to slow down ships and weaken piers. There are, of course, different types of barnacles. Weirdly enough, these are crustaceans (same group as crabs and shrimps!), part of a class called Cirripedia (meaning 'hairy foot'). This is what Hermit Crab saw when she went to deliver a welcome treat.

Just like she did, if it's alive, you will see what the late B.F. Chhapgar described perfectly, in his book on shore life, as a tiny volcano. This flattened top has a slit, acting like a lined door. When not submerged in water, this is tightly closed. When the water flows over it, the slit opens, and cirri (feathery legs) emerge. They look like gnarled hands, or tentacles even, but are actually the animal's legs coming out to feed, filtering its meal through the water. It strongly reminded me of those games we played where you had to fix the magnet on a fish set on a rotating board, that opened and closed its mouth at regular intervals. If it's dead, you'll probably cut yourself on its jagged top if you slip and make contact.

Barnacles have four life stages. Nauplius is the free-floating larval stage. Once it finds its home, a barnacle larva secretes a

---

* Captain Archibald Haddock is a fictional character in The Adventures of Tintin, the comics series by Hergé. He uses a number of colourful curses, of which the most well known is 'billions of blue blistering barnacles!'

glue-like substance and attaches itself head first onto the rock. This is the cyprid stage where the animal first uses a reversible adhesive while exploring the substrate for a suitable site. Once it finds it, it uses a stronger adhesive called cyprid cement to colonize the substrate. Then there are the juvenile and adult sessile stages. At the juvenile and adult stages, it uses something called barnacle cement for permanent adhesion. This is so strong that the barnacle remains attached to the substrate even after its death. It buys into it for life (and beyond). None of that renting nonsense, no 'guess I'll give it a try'.

The home it builds is a hard shell-like hillock, made of a variable number of plates — and lives ensconced inside it. When it wants to feed, a slit opens up on the surface and its legs pop out to catch food. When it's not submerged in water, it folds its feet inside, shuts the slit tight and waits it out. It literally puts its best foot forward for sustenance.

Naveen Namboothri is a fan of the barnacle. He said, 'Barnacles are not overtly into exorbitant ornamentation, the design is so minimalistic. It spends its energies smartly.' He added:

> Also, they're open to predation but compensate by creating many offspring. They're capable of living even in places where there is human interference; they might even benefit from it. Those are the ones that are going to make it in the long run. The more a species gets into specialisation, into a specific behavioural adaption or a habitat requirement, you'll be on the losing end of the evolutionary spectrum.

That's a lesson right there for us as well. Naveen's PhD thesis was on the unfortunately named 'boring organisms'. He wanted to write about the Lithotrya, rock-boring, stalked barnacles, only to find that Darwin of all people had beaten him to it. Darwin worked on barnacles for eight years, after which he famously said, 'I hate a barnacle as no man ever did before, not even a sailor in a slow-moving ship.'

I had new respect for the humble barnacle after it brazenly got down to business right in front of us on a walk.

We were at a tide pool in Mumbai, and a barnacle opened its slit and an appendage snaked out. I assumed this is the usual, 'I am eating with my feet, why are you staring' situation. But instead of collecting particles from the water and taking them inside, the appendage started to feel along the tide pool, extending to an unexpected length, until it found another barnacle. As the latter opened, our fellow inserted this appendage, which I now know was its rather long penis, into the other individual. Hardt's *Sex in the Sea* has gems like this: 'If there were a penis Olympics, the following species [barnacle] would win the decathlon, sporting not only the world's longest proportional penis, but also a remarkably agile and malleable one.' That's quite a rave review. Although, studies argue that long, thin penises often do not work as well as short, thick ones. Apparently because the longer ones can get dragged around more than the shorter ones. Too much information, Barnacles, behave. On an average, Dr Chhapgar says, a single barnacle will bring forth 9000 young every year.

It's always the silent, innocuous-looking ones that turn out to be the weirdest, no?

Bryozoans — Clones with Personalities

While the others can colonize shores by cloning and spawning, the bryozoan takes this game to the next level. Bryozoans are commonly known as 'moss animals' — that's what their name translates to. If you, like me, balked at the oxymoron, it's not about the constitution of the animal, but where it lives. They look like moss and live in habitats where you would expect to find moss. Bryozoans are mistaken for almost everything else — sponges, coral, hydroids, seaweed and even cloth or plastic. They're a bit obscure, not entirely in the glam kingdom of popular animals. They're not seen everywhere on a shore — they need niche areas and shaded rock pools. They cannot live in open spaces that have no small nooks and too much movement. They're not well studied either, but work on them in India is slowly growing. For example, Mahi Mankeshwar has found fifty-seven decidedly different species in Ratnagiri, but has successfully identified only twenty to twenty-five so far.

They can make their own colony, yes, but every clone can play a *separate* role. Imagine you're a Bryozoan larva, happily floating around the intertidal zone. You like a beautiful, rocky, shady area. Like the barnacle, you settle in. So you start building your home. The skeleton structure of a Bryozoan colony is made from calcium, which you, also called an individual 'zooid', secrete yourself. Then you feel ready to start a colony so you multiply: yes, *clone yourself into many zooids and start living a merry, Bollywood-level large family life.* All you zooids, which form the animals of the colony, will belong to different types and will serve different functions and modify the colony — feeding, protection, generate spines or flaps to keep slugs away. So they are clones, but with specific, individual jobs. The level of strategy from something this tiny!

Like sea sponges, they're sometimes a foundation species, meaning they're usually the first to arrive after an algal biofilm, which is like a gateway to a settlement. A biofilm is a thin film of microbes that settled before it, and provided a foundation for other creatures like coral, barnacles, bryozoans and the rest. They are the original settlers and other creatures will find sustenance on it.

There's also just the scale of it all. Naveen says:

> More than 90 per cent have a larval dispersal stage — from massive fish like tuna to tiny corals or sponges. And they disperse widely. That is what makes me hopeful in the case of marine ecosystems, they are more resilient than forest systems. They can really bounce back if you let them. The scales and speed at which they can bounce back is more satisfying to see than a terrestrial system. But again, it's not easy to facilitate the process of restoration because there is so much we don't know yet about this ecosystem. That is why our lens cannot be restricted to biology, it has to extend to physics and hydro-dynamics to understand where dispersal is taking place and how, depending on tides, currents and waves. There is a long way to go.

The superpower perhaps common in all animals is the focus on propagating their species. Shaunak Modi, a citizen scientist interested in intertidal ecology, and a member of Marine Life of Mumbai, was tidepooling in Malvan and saw a female crab carrying her eggs under her. He watched as she became aware of a male crab and began to hide from him constantly as he approached. She scurried away under a rock and waited. 'We wondered what she would do now', Shaunak remembers. He adds:

> So we waited as well. She was in a deep corner of the crevice. She was shuffling constantly. We waited for 45 minutes, just sitting with her and watching. As the tide turned, the water reached. She was still. A giant wave rose and flowed over the rock, flowed over her, and when the water receded, we saw in shock that the

eggs were gone. She had released them. I was so humbled in that moment — how she had positioned herself, escaped other creatures, knowing what spot to hide out so she could release her eggs. She did what was best for her babies.

It was at that moment that Shaunak paused on the shore. He recalls running from pool to pool to see more creatures, to take more photos, but the rewards of staying still around a creature are immense — and being around one that's making new life is priceless.

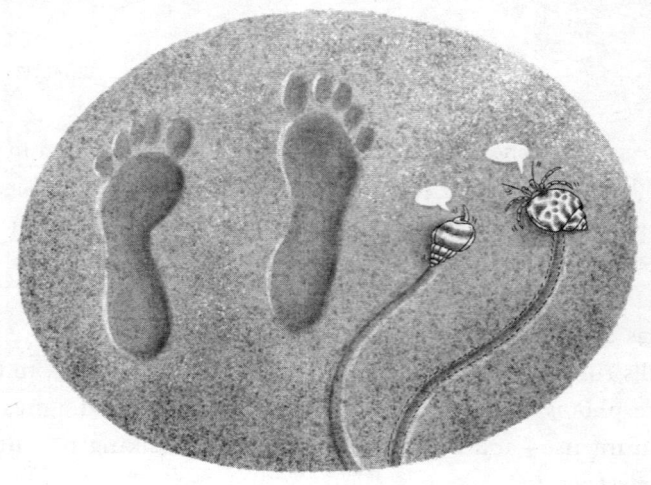

A SIMPLE ACT
OF WALKING—AN
EXERCISE IN SEEING

Walking is falling forward.

    Each step we take is an arrested plunge, a collapse averted, a disaster braked. In this way, to walk becomes an act of faith. We perform it daily: a two-beat miracle—an iambic teetering, a holding on and letting go. For the next seven years I will plummet across the world.

                        —Paul Salopek, journalist

When you walk somewhere, your entire being is present in the moment. As Salopek said, it is a two-beat miracle. Putting one foot in front of the other literally and figuratively tethers us to the present. While his quest involves a journey of about 33,800 kilometres, and stories and findings about the world we inhabit, closer home, the writer and film-maker Siddharth Agarwal is walking along India's rivers to document the twists and turns they share with people. In West Bengal, two marathon runners, Avisek Tunga and Debabrata Ghosh, ran along the 55-kilometre intertidal region from Bankitput to Digha, in a campaign to raise awareness about the coastline. They ran over the wet sand, waded across river systems, spoke to fishers and saw a wild intertidal zone at dawn.

I never really thought that the simple act of walking on a shore can be this vital.

In Mumbai, Gopal M.S., called 'Slogan Murugan' and 'Mumbai Paused' on social media, is a city documenter. He started to capture the city in photographs, not to any end, but to make sense of where he lived, and gradually to record what it meant. The slowest form of photography, he said, was to sit in one spot while the action happened around you. Conversation happens when you stop, stay and sit, when you exchange food or water and stories. The next is walking. When you walk, you are able to observe things, people and moments.

What do you see when you walk? On a beach, this might mean watching the sand, or the cute candy crush-like umbonium sea snails — pink, chocolate brown, peach or maroon — doing what appears like backflips when disturbed. Or it could mean looking up at the catch the fisher's pulled in. Or it could mean looking at the houses that overlook the beaches, with balconies that promise sunsets accompanied with tea. Or the houses that fall close to the gradually advancing high tideline, now within buffeting range of the monsoon storms. Or the woman bent over the rocks with a sickle breaking open oysters (or *kalva* as we say in Marathi). On the Lakshadweep islands, it could mean a community, social interaction for women as they hunt octopuses in ankle-deep water. On tourist shores across the world, it could mean watching the evening rush, people talking over video calls, showing their loved ones back home the magnificent ocean. Or it might mean spotting the candy sellers and the balloon sellers. The beach is a place of leisure, it is a place of business, it is a place of livelihood and it is a home. And it is different from shore to shore.

Siddharth Chakravarty, one of the initial founders of Marine Life in Mumbai, before he left to study and understand coastal policies, is a strong advocate for learning through conversation — and in the simplest of ways. He had gone for a run at a beach in West Bengal, and noticed some glistening shapes at the water's edge. Closer inspection revealed heaps and heaps of stranded box jellyfish. He struck up a conversation with a fisher who referred to them as *telfotka*, which translates to 'oil droplet' because of the creature's appearance. 'They become like oil and clog up the nets', the fisher said, 'so we're not fishing right now'. Siddharth asked him when he would be able to fish again, and he replied, 'When the wind changes direction. When it blows these animals away, we can take the boats out again.' He was surprised because this usually never happens in February, 'so something is up with the weather'. What a simple conversation and yet so much said about people and the intertidal zone, climate change and history.

Historian Sandeep Dahisarkar writes about a walking ground that has impacted history in a piece titled *Of Kings and Coconuts and Juhu's First Family.* He writes about walks on Juhu beach taken by none other than Mahatma Gandhi, who was known to frequent its sandy tidelines when he lived in the city in the 1900s. It also went on to be a significant ally of sorts during the salt satyagraha. Between 1899 and 1904, while under the British rule, Juhu was the site of an interesting plan by Jamsetji Tata. He planned to criss-cross the islands and mudflats with canals. Historian R.M. Lala writes about it in his book, *For the Love of India: The Life and Times of Jamsetji Tata.* The plan was to use 1,200 acres of the shore and demarcate it into canals and plots, so the tide could play a role in the water supply. The idea, which came to be known as the 'Venice Scheme', never did take root due to differences in opinions from landowners.

You might drive along shores, snorkel in the shallows and dive in the deep and you'll learn different things, past and present. One day, when the sea had retreated farther inside (which it does during an extremely low tide) I walked onto the sandy section of Juhu beach, a shore I thought I knew so well, to see tiny plateaus rising out of the water. This is the part of the beach where large boulders are usually hidden from sight underwater. These were revealed on the lowest of tides. I watched as people walked on the boulders, accidentally tidepooling, watching crabs, eels, and watching fisherwomen collect clams — all of this right on the most crowded, touristy part of the beach.

Walking along an intertidal zone is also the act of being able to walk up to a sea creature and stay with it until the tide returns. Once, on a late evening in Juhu, we saw a live sea fan (a type of soft coral) anchored in the sand when the light had already left. It was like something I'd only seen in documentaries, or like the dead ones that wash onto the beach. Under the torchlight, it seemed to exist in another galaxy, the water particles like tiny stars lit around it. To be able to walk up to this strange animal that looks every bit like a tiny tree but is very much an animal, and then sit with it at leisure with a macro lens and observe the tiniest skeleton shrimps (as large as one-third of my fingernail) perched on it — that's powerful, isn't it? Because you'd usually see sea fans just in the deep. Ram Vilas Ghosh, a researcher who has been working on these animals for four years, was gobsmacked when he came across them in Maharashtra's intertidal zone. 'They usually need pristine water, what are they doing in Mumbai?' he said, delighted. He remembers a conversation with fishers in Tamil Nadu. They'd caught a gorgonian sea fan in their net, and were ignoring it because they assumed, like everyone does, that it's a plant. Ghosh smiled and said:

> When a sea fan is submerged in water, you can see its real power. . . . It literally blossoms and those colours are just incredible. I took it to the water and showed them that this was a sea creature, not a plant and their excitement and wonder was palpable. This changed their view entirely for future sightings. This is why we must walk, must work with people and exchange our learnings [*sic*].

Yes, empathy is a valuable characteristic — the more you walk, the more careful you are with marine life on the shores. Photographers, if you feel the need to move your subject around simply because you can, for 'that' particular photograph, hone your craft and do better. We have to realize that our interest in them and the way we engage with them could cost them energy, or worse, a predatory attack. They are in the middle of their day when I am watching them. If they are in the middle of a hunt or being hunted, any carelessness from me could cost them either a meal or their lives. Leave things as they are, and don't carry things home; everything gets used up, even homes. On a shore in Karwar, I saw a whole patch of rocks covered with honeycomb-like tubes — and the name fit. They were homes made by the honeycomb worm, but after its death, it inadvertently leaves a network of homes for so many more things.

The sign of a superpower is that it empowers others.

And your mind starts to think more inclusively about the definition of what it means. When we think of wildlife, we often only think of pristine forests and protected areas. This fraction alone cannot, and does not, support all wildlife. We need to expand our lens beyond areas that are protected by law. Wild animals do not recognize administrative boundaries. Many of these habitats — not just forests, but deserts, grasslands, wetlands and coasts — are vital for humans and wildlife alike, whether they belong in urban, semi-urban or rural areas. All of this needs our respect and empathy, not just protected areas. It just reiterates that wilderness is only where a wild animal stays, not a boundary that we get to set.

It's truer than ever for a coast, isn't it? In 2019, I was in Malvan to listen to dolphins. I was on an assignment for Mongabay India, to write about Isha Bopardikar's research on understanding dolphin behaviour through acoustic data under the Rufford Foundation's 'Small Grant for Nature Conservation'. Acoustic research uses sound to study subjects; bioacoustics tucks biology into that fold. Simply put, it is used to listen, and understand their communication and behaviour. Under the water, early-morning bulletins were already underway; we just weren't invited to the conversation. But humans have been gate crashing wildlife parties for centuries, so there we were, waiting to eavesdrop on the latest news. It reiterated how little we actually hear, despite the constant cacophony around us. Whether it is bats in the skies or this entire civilization under the water, so many creatures communicate through mediums and frequencies humans are categorically excluded from.

And just like in the shallows and the deep, life and sound unfolds at Malvan's shore. It is a sensory splash: cars, bikes, horses, horse carts, water sports vehicles, boats, fishing boats, fish auctions, ice factories, crates, and every single thing surviving at the water's edge. Plus, there is the contribution of a bustling intertidal zone.

All in the same place.

Our residence was a small, two-storied house with rooms dedicated to researchers staying for months on end, cooking their meals, poring over data sheets, and prepping for field day (which means a day out in the field, and not necessarily a fabulous day). On the mornings when we'd visit the beach, we would step out right on to the beach with a cup of tea, something a Mumbai girl does not take lightly, and would meet the absolutely bizarre Arabian tibia, a sea snail that if you see up-close looks like it has a trunk. The fringed sea star (*Astropecten indicus*) spread out and wriggled its way in and out of the sand, and the occasional sea snake was waiting for the water to wash it back in.

Research suggests that the negative ions around the shores actually help our bodies feel better. A forest's embrace is a comforting thing, as is the ocean's reliable presence. The flowers and the earth are fragrant. The beach is fragrant too; when Kramer wanted to bottle the smell of the beach in *Seinfeld*, he was really on to something. Memories are such a sensory experience. If I think of the shore, I automatically smell the salt, the slightly humid feeling, sulphur, and yes, even poop.

Of all the things strange and wonderful about scientists, their capacity to discuss poop is remarkable. Leopard scat, tiger scat, elephant dung—the list is endless. While on a writing assignment on otters, I am certain there was lots of pointing and laughing from the river as we sat around their poop to understand their dietary habits. As a tidepooler (someone who actively looks into tide pools for intertidal animals), unfortunately, you might have to add human poop to that list.

But what does your body do when it walks repeatedly on a shore? It understands. On a sandy beach, it relaxes, and it is almost playful. On a muddy one, it anticipates the squelching, knows you might sink several inches into the muck, and it prepares for it. Go to a rocky shore, and your body tenses, anticipating an undulating climb. There are slippery boulders and sharp barnacles—your body moves to protect you from hurting yourself. All your senses are present. Ah, don't step on those shells, don't hurt the shrimps— your body's memory avoids stomping across the tide pools just because they promise flatter ground. After four years, I am proof that a body not only sees, but also remembers.

Walking is meditative and introspective. It is the best teacher we have about ourselves, and the concept of change. Walking leads to new perspectives. Various conversations reveal small truths about the city and the shore. Each conversation is like a piece in a large jigsaw. With every piece, one more thing about your backyard clicks into place.

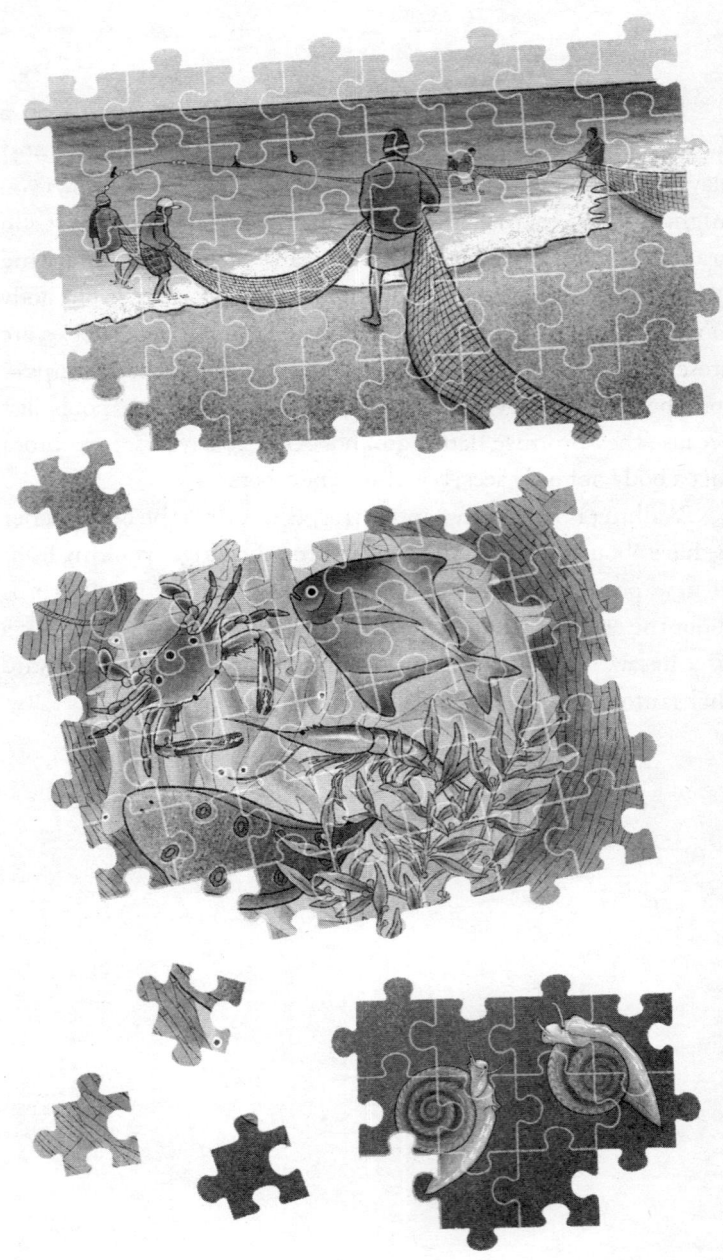

The best puzzles click into place slowly,

over time and exploration

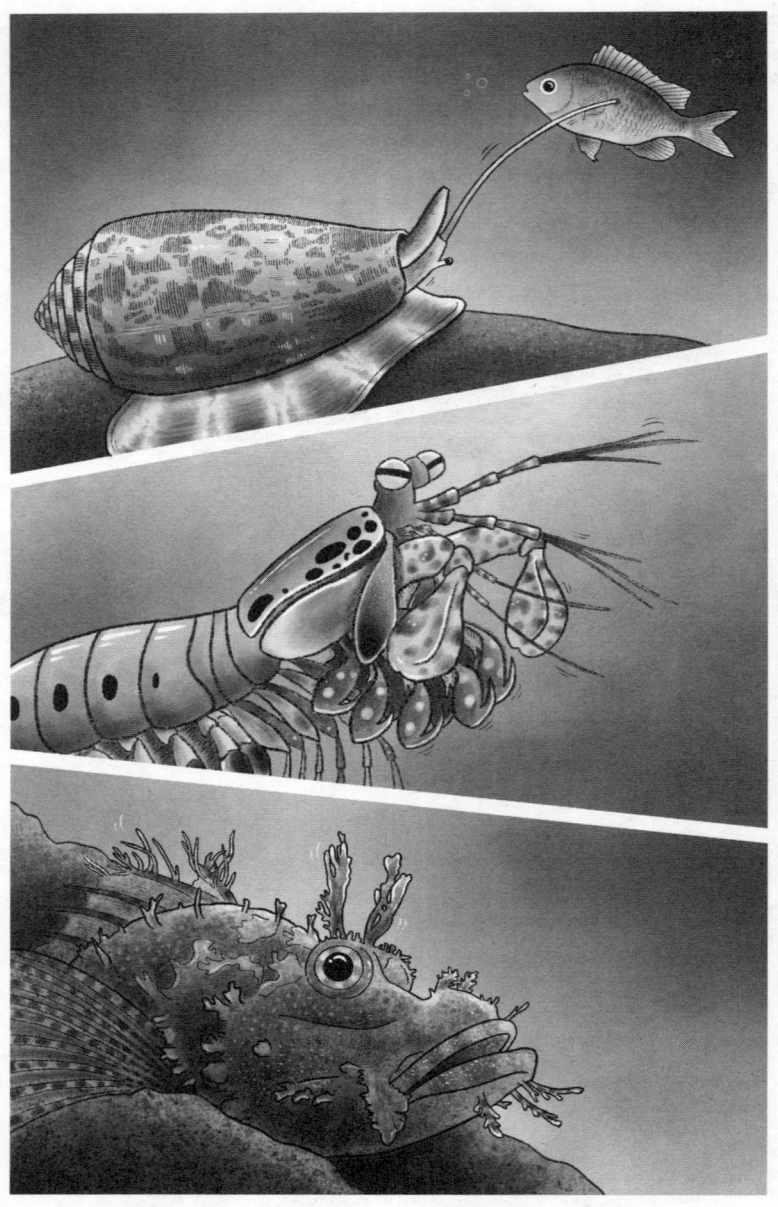

From top: A cone snail's harpoon finds its mark; the mantis shrimp and its Hulk impression; a scorpionfish waits, armed and deadly

6

ASSASSINS OF THE INTERTIDAL

TOXINS, HARPOONS, BRUTE FORCE

School's out for the day. Hermit Crab is taking last roll call.
She teaches at the school at the corner of her neighbourhood
tide pool.
She sends off the tiny fish, sea snails sooner.
It's almost dusk, predators will be out, like smooth assassins
looking for their meal.
As the evening light starts to fade, a sea snail on the rocky
intertidal (by now you should be throwing this word
around like a pro) begins to stir.

Shaped like a cone, its shell lends the snail its name. The cone snail is slow, but deadly, one of the few known animals in this landscape that could be fatal to humans, too.

It's time to prep for dinner.

Hermit Crab ensures everyone has reached safely and leaves school.

She scuttles quickly, in comparison to the cone snail, which moves slowly by pushing out its one large foot, typical of all gastropods.

Hermit Crab sees the fish just as the cone snail does.

The cone snail glides closer, slowly feeling and sniffing around with its siphon to track its prey. But it's the fourth appendage that's truly one of the deadliest superpowers on the intertidal.

The proboscis, a tube-like organ alongside the siphon, conceals a lethal weapon at its tip: a harpoon that is loaded with venom made of potent neurotoxins for which there is no known antidote.

Hermit Crab calls out to the fish to warn him. But the fish pays her no heed.

When it gets close enough, the cone snail shoots the harpoon from the proboscis at the fish, injecting the neurotoxins that paralyse the animal. Backward-pointing barbs get stuck in the flesh.

The cone snail reels the fish in, and then swallows it whole.

Hermit Crab shudders at the mouth that distends like an anaconda.

She walks away. This is the way of the intertidal, she thinks. Eat or be eaten.

~

Y ou think you know your shores well?

Do you know that silent battles are fought here?

At these spaces where the sun paints the sky, battle lines are drawn and swept away under the watery veil of the blue ocean.

At this coast, where you escape to introspect about the tiny discomforts of your lives, a daily ritual of death plays out. Not once, not twice, but numerous times. And yet, while assassins prowl here, and there is venom and weaponry, a fight to the death has never been more well intentioned as it is in nature. In most cases, animals take what they need, no more or less than that. Nature has checks in place for the large part. Did you know then that this beach you thought you knew so well was, in truth, a battlefield without a single villain in the war?

We're naturally attracted to the idea of predators. Nature documentaries that are full of jaws and claws and teeth get top billing on networks. The roar of a big cat in a forest thrills us to the bone, as does the panicked cry of its prey. Isn't our reaction to an alarm call in a forest a strange irony? An animal, for example, like a spotted deer or a langur, calls when it is in danger, and sounds an alarm to warn others. As supposedly upstanding citizens of society, we are brought up to value life, all life, human and otherwise. But when we hear an alarm call ring out in the forest, in essence, we know something is in danger, and is probably dying. Yet, we turn our safari vehicles in chase of the source. We stare wide-eyed, crazed on adrenaline, hoping to see a 'natural history' moment that might be an animal's last.

Yes, predators thrill us. This is why streaming platforms make a killing (excuse the pun) on serial killer documentaries or crime dramas. In 2020, when most of us only had access to the world through media, documentaries collected the most eyeballs on streaming platforms, with the true crime shows topping the statistics. Our shadow selves are in morbid curiosity and awe over someone who stepped out of what is acceptable in human society and stole someone's most precious possession — their life.

While wildlife safaris in the forest are exciting, and I recommend them to every single one of you, look closer home for these moments as well. Our backyards, shores and gardens are teeming with predators, gifted with the most astonishing powers, harpoons, speed, sharp teeth, and so much more. Everywhere is a wildlife documentary, if only you care to look.

A Cone, Venom, and a Laboratory

Cone snails (under the genus *Conus*) have always evoked awe in me. The fact that from all the creatures in the intertidal zone, some relatives of this snail have been documented (albeit rarely) to have been fatal to humans who disturb it, makes it even more powerful.

Also, you'd think the way it hunts is the coolest thing it can do. Well, you'd be wrong.

Remember Hawkeye from the Marvel universe?* This is how a conversation between them would go:

'Hawkeye: I literally have a boomerang arrow that returns to me, so I don't ever have to technically run out.

Conus: Bro, hold my beer.'

Essentially, many species of snails can regrow their teeth. They experience wear and tear while using theirs, and can regenerate lost teeth. Some carnivorous snails use toxic secretions too, but the

---

* Hawkeye is a superhero from the Marvel comics universe. Created by Stan Lee and Don Heck in 1964.

cone snail comes with the added innovation of actively using its venom-laced tooth as a harpoon.*

The venom of a cone snail has at least 500 different components in its venom, perhaps more now. It is actually able to construct a different type of venom that flows into the harpoon *each time*, depending on the usage, hunt or defence. It's like making an individual potion for each arrow inside its own little mind's laboratory: a bit of this, a bit of that, oh, let's throw this in as well. There are more than 500 species of venomous cone snails, so that's at least 2,50,000 permutations and combinations. That is why it's difficult to find an antidote.

Plus, it never runs out of venom-filled harpoons.

This assassin is also known to burrow in the sand, unseen until a fish gets close enough for the nastiest and final surprise of its life.

As Professor Jaime Seymour, who works on cone snails, says, 'If it's a cone, leave it alone.' Human superheroes, please sit down.

The arsenals of the creatures in the intertidal zone are incredible to fathom. From spears to harpoons and stingers to brute force, or even smothering other animals to death, they're singularly skilled in their ability to catch prey.

The ribbon worm prowls the intertidal zone with a spearing device of its own. Thin and long as its name suggests, this worm is capable of extending and retracting its body when threatened. The deep-sea cousin in the ribbon worm group is the *Lineus longissimus*, which is known as one of the longest animals on earth, reaching lengths of 50 metres! Of course, in the tide pool, it's smaller in scale, but an interesting sight nonetheless, gliding

---

* *How Killer Cone Snails Kill*, The *Nature of Science*, produced with the assistance of the James Cook University, https://www.youtube.com/watch?v=4wihKnARrAw&t=34.

in the water or slithering over the rocks with grace. The ribbon worm belongs to the phylum Nemertea, and certain species have remarkably potent toxins. It has an eversible proboscis that it uses to catch its prey and reel it in. The proboscis has sticky papillae (structures on the tongue that give it the rough texture). The precision of this action is such that it never misses. I have, on numerous occasions, accidentally taken a screenshot on my phone while merely wanting to increase the volume, so advanced motor skills are very attractive to me.

Spear or Smash — A Strategy of Brute Force

Spearing is quite the popular form of attack in the marine realm. But wait. Despite the clean segue from the harpoon to the spear, let me take a second to say, this animal's superpowers boggle the mind, so strap in, as things are going to get wild.

Along the intertidal zone, usually under the cover of water, lives the mantis shrimp, an animal that gets its name from the insect (the praying mantis) because of the shared stance they adopt: claws joined in prayer. But when it fights, that's when it becomes a kung fu film protagonist.

There are two kinds of mantis shrimps — appropriately named spearers and smashers. The distinction is based on their food appendages, meaning that decides what they eat. Spearers will attack softer prey, like fishes, squids or octopuses. They lie in wait, and when the prey gets near, they swiftly pounce and spear the animal with the sharp, hook-like spines on their claws — think of Okoye in Marvel's *Black Panther*.

The other group of mantis shrimps are smashers, like a version of the Hulk of the intertidal zone, and they use good old-fashioned brute force. Though sea stars also use strength to pry open clams and other animals, the mantis shrimp uses force to clobber. Their claws have knobs that they use to punch their prey (they are even able to crack open shells) or to defend themselves against other animals.

Its fight stance is the 'meral spread': it stands like a boxer in its corner, 'arms' wide and the meral spots visible. This warns any predator that it's prepared to fight, and boy, can it fight. The mantis shrimp can thump even larger animals. In fact, a marine researcher, Tanmay Wagh, got his thumb walloped by a mantis shrimp while poking around under the rocks in the Andaman Islands.

And it's not much of a contest when the mantis decides to hunt. The mantis shrimp is built for the kill, to use the oft-repeated cliché. They even have superpower vision that uses sixteen receptors as opposed to our three, which allows them to see more keenly than any of us or any other animal for that matter. This allows them to tap into ultraviolet and infrared wavelengths. New research has helped in facilitating a camera based on the eye of the mantis shrimp that can help in the detection of tumours and cancer cells, and even assist in surgeries. All of these combined powers make them one of the most efficient predators in the intertidal zones. I would not like to get into a boxing ring with a mantis shrimp.

The Fastest Trigger This Side of the Intertidal

Its cousin, on the other hand, wields energy with its hands. If you have visited a rocky shore, you've heard this one, even if you haven't seen it. Listen for small pops, little short sounds that, try as you might, you can't locate the source of. That's the pistol shrimp.

Now, with a name like that, its modus operandi is rather obvious, and yet terrifying. It is like a cowboy in a tide pool. Pistol shrimps are excellent burrowers. If you watch one in action, what you'll see is a cloud of mud created by five pairs of swimming legs furiously kicking up sand, almost looking like the exhaust smoke of a revving motorcycle.

Camouflaged and able to move with speed, in reverse and whatnot, this one is a perfect assassin. It glides over rocks with expertise; even if we could hear underwater, it would seem like it's tiptoeing. Ironic, because they're such noisemakers — they're notorious for interfering with bioacoustics research for deep-sea animals, like the loudest people at a party.

Let's go to the source of all its powers: the unique mechanics of its oversized claws. Abhishek explains this gunslinger's weaponry:

When the shrimp opens the big claw, the movable 'thumb' of the claw locks in the open position, like the spring-loaded hammer of a revolver. When snapped shut, the force of this motion sends forward a high-speed jet of water, with a backward roll-up of water in a ring around this jet's fringes. Sounds complicated? The roll-up itself is simple everyday physics that you can check out right now — move your hand through a tub of water, and you can see it as short-lived whirlpools, spinning in a 'backward' sense either side of the path your hand traced. These modest-looking whirlpools are the two free ends of a semi-circular, U-shaped underwater roll-up your hand created. But with this shrimp's super-fast water jet, the accompanying roll-up (ring-shaped here, because the shrimp's shooting motion is entirely underwater, not interrupted by the water surface) happens with such speed that the ring vortex rapidly loses pressure and turns into an air bubble ring. When the bubble collapses, it does so with a pressure pulse strong enough to stun or kill a small animal.

This is about the closest thing to a fireball underwater, which is perhaps even more impressive.

This bubble creates a loud 'POP' that can go as high as 210 decibels at the source, and that's what you're hearing. The cacophony from vast colonies of pistol shrimps firing these bubbles has even been known to disrupt underwater sonar equipment.

'What Big Teeth You Have, Grandma'

Gastropods play the role of the herbivores from the forest. The way that deer and other grazers keep the grass in check, by eating it, these creatures manage the intertidal zone in this manner. They keep the algal growth in check, which can otherwise overpower substrates, and allow nothing else to grow there. Herbivorous radula looks a bit like a chainsaw. If you imagined it in actual human size, it is the stuff nightmares are made of. Rows and rows of razor-sharp teeth sit on its tongue, called the radula; they are made of a strong substance called chitin. With these tiny knives on its tongue, it starts to scrape the algae off the rocks. You watch in awe and gratitude, both for the meal and for the fact that the gastropods on our shores are tiny.

Now, of course, it wouldn't be enough for the animal to just have this power. The universe looked at its sharp mouth and thought, 'I need some more to work with here, let's ramp this up.' The teeth are sharp and are replaceable. Predatory snails in the intertidal zone have evolved to use their radula to kill. They have evolved alongside their prey.

Certain species of limpets possess teeth that are made from the strongest biological material known to humans. This super-material is a composite of chitin and goethite (an iron-based mineral), which can match up to the power of some of the strongest man-made materials — including those used in bulletproof vests and aerospace structures!

Different species have different types of radula — for example, a herbivore needs a rough tongue to scrape algae off the jagged rock surfaces. The carnivores, on the other hand, have different arsenals. The moon snail is a monster to its prey.* It has one of the prettier shells because it has a mantle (a covering) that keeps it shiny and doesn't allow encrusting animals to start growing on it. They make very pretty egg sacs. The next time, keep an eye out on a sandy beach for these: they look like the top half of a collared shirt or the top half of an earthen pot — miniscule versions of course.

Like most sea snails, the moon snail has a large, muscular foot with which it moves around.

But this creature, which otherwise could be around 2 centimetres, can grow to a monstrous size that is several times the size of its shell, by inflating its tissue with seawater. It is like a very slowly transforming Hulk. It uses this larger foot to first smother its prey. Then out come the big guns — it uses its radula to drill holes into the shells of gastropods or bivalves, and the tip of its proboscis has a gland that secretes acid. 'Think of a hard cardboard that you want to cut through', says Abhishek, as we follow the smooth progress of this animal. It's the smoothest glider, its body designed to plough through the sand it's going through. Abhishek adds, 'If you wet the cardboard a bit, it's easier to drill through. That's what the snail is doing to the shell.' It's a bit of a perfectionist too; you can tell that a moon snail has reached its prey by just looking at the perfect hole it's made. It uses this to soften the hard shell of the animal before making a perfectly

---

* http://www.wildsingapore.com/wildfacts/mollusca/gastropoda/naticidae/naticidae.htm.

round hole, and then it slurps up its contents like a nice slurpee on a hot afternoon.

Yes, we're fortunate they're tiny.

Step back Lake Placid, here's a candidate for a new monster movie — a marine snail.

And the next animal is a perfect actor to join the cast.

Ambush and a Death Hug

Hermit Crab was waiting for her friend, Nassa Mud Snail.

They were to go to an art exhibition.

The sand bubbler crabs were doing something new with their pellets.

Hermit Crab had always admired their artistry.

How they could dig out sand, filter their food from it and make a rangoli from the pellets.

How cool and how very sustainable.

Hermit Crab checked the time.

She checked to see if the rock and coral patch was the same that they had decided upon.

It was. This Nassa Mud Snail was always late.

They needed to reach before the tide turned.

She rolled her eyes and leaned back on the rock, sighing.

To her shock, the rock moved and spoke.

'Do you mind', said the long-suffering scorpionfish, as Hermit Crab keeled over and fell.

A few fish jumped in alarm and left.

'Honestly!' said the irritated fish. 'You have just blown my cover. I've been here for hours! HOURS! Now I'll have to start over.'

As Hermit Crab gathered herself and tried to right herself, the scorpionfish swam away in a huff.

Hermit Crab finally sat up, shaken and wide-eyed.
Never trusting Nassa Mud Snail with maps again. Ever.

~

The scorpionfish is an ambush predator with a supreme skill set. They're masters of camouflage. They are the actual manifestation of 'good things come to those who wait' and so on and so forth. They can sit still for hours — they are a lesson in patience. They blend in perfectly with coral-encrusting rocks, and when the prey is close enough, they lunge forward and engulf it whole. They're venomous creatures, adding another level of trauma to their victims.

And the final nail in the coffin is its defence mechanism — thirteen spines on their dorsal fin that is capable of shooting venom in all directions. While it's super effective in the intertidal zone, it's also a fair warning to humans.

Marine biologist Vardhan Patankar was in the Nicobar Islands when he saw how severely painful this could be. The village captain mistakenly stepped on one and he wept in pain. Patankar recounts:

> I administered vinegar and warm water as first-aid because the former is protein. It was fine in a few days but walking the intertidal, you need to watch where you step or what you hold. It's a gorgeous creature, and an interesting species but dangerous, too.

In terms of ambush predators, I'd still prefer the scorpionfish to what's coming next. If I were a marine creature, I'd be absolutely terrified of the bobbit worm. It's the kind of thing we'd be warned about as children, and the areas that it inhabited would be placed off limits by our parents. It's like something out of *The X-Files* that everyone knows exists and no one wants to acknowledge or talk about.

Let me paint you a horrifying picture: you're a fish, swimming along the shallows, zipping here and there, oblivious that among the open tentacles of the colourful anemones and the festive headgear of a feather duster worm, lies a creature from your worst nightmares.

You see a few tentacles on the sea floor, flattened against a—wait, is that a mouth—WHAM!

Before you can cry out 'MUMMY!', a long shape rises, like a snake out of the seabed, and gets you. Here's the terrifying thing about this creature: a bobbit worm is long and hides most of its

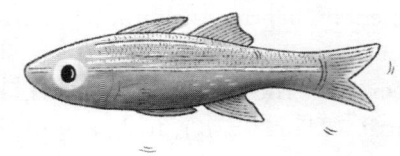

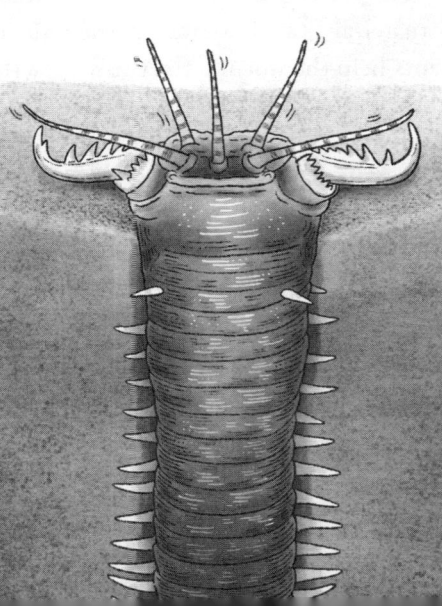

body buried under the soft seabed, with only its tentacles and mouth out.

This worm rushes out at you and its razor-sharp jaws can slice a creature clean in half with a speed that's almost too quick to anticipate. The rest of the body is like a U-shaped funnel in the sand. The length of its body is something you didn't even know was there. It's like finding the face of an eel and realizing it's an anaconda in the water. For something less sinister but also charming, it's just waiting there, but holding out a deathly hug.

Of course, survival finds a way. Recent research found how fish rallied around their comrades. They would mob the predator, blowing jets of water at it if one of theirs was caught. It does something vital — it exposes the predator's location, and once it loses the element of surprise, the game's no longer one-sided.

There is a worm that remains invisible by literally doing the opposite: decorating. The shell-binder worms, also aptly known as decorator worms (*Diopatra sp.*), are burrowing polychaete worms found on our sandy beaches, often in the thousands. They secrete a parchment-like tube around themselves and 'decorate' this with bits of solid material that they find in their surroundings. The embellishments help the worm attract tiny prey that it can then feed on. As the name suggests, the bits used are usually shell pieces, but it's common to see plastic and all sorts of other trash too.

A Net for a Hood

The other animal to completely take you by surprise is the *Melibe* sea slug. I have watched Elastigirl in *The Incredibles* with no small amount of envy. How easy it would be to just use our bodies to extend and retract at will, to be able to traverse outside of our spaces, outside windows and over rooftops. Reality, of course, continues to

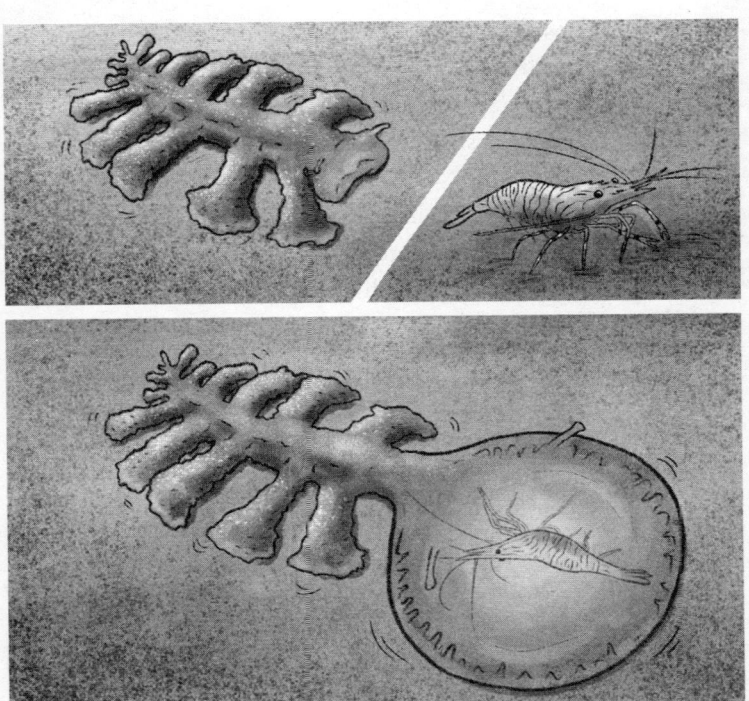

The *Melibe sp.* sea slug: gone fishin' with a head net

ruin my life, à la Bill Waterson, when I can't even reach for my TV remote a few feet away. In that, maybe these are small mercies. If I had this power, I'd probably never move again.

The *Melibe sp.* nudibranch is blessed with a strange power. Imagine a sea slug with eight extensions on the side. Like a fisher out in the intertidal zone, this slug walks along the seabed, and when faced with potential prey, is able to expand and throw a part of its own body out on the prey like a fishing net!

Can you imagine this? It catches prey inside a fishing net made of its own head. Apparently, this animal, over the course of evolution, has lost its radula, and hence uses an oral veil (think of an astronaut but with a bulbous, transparent and fluid bubble. This veil has tiny hair-like projections all along its margin, and when it senses small prey like a shrimp or crab, it casts its net and devours the creature.

In the deep waters of our oceans, a wondrous phenomenon called 'whale fall' happens when the animal dies.

When a whale dies, it literally falls to the depths, and in the process, becomes a form of sustenance for so many lives for years to come.

Yes, for years.

First come the larger predators — the fish and the sharks which can feed on the colossal carcass for two years! Then come the smaller creatures — the worms, crustaceans and molluscs which feed on the blubber and burrow into the flesh of the body. According to a piece in the Smithsonian:

> The final stage, called the sulfophilic (literally meaning sulpher lovers) stage, can last decades. With only the skeleton remaining, bacteria begin breaking down lipids trapped inside the bones, generating sulpher, which attracts more bacteria and a larger community of diverse species including mussels, worms, snails, and others. This diversity of species found in this last stage is larger than any known community on the deep seafloor.*

This is how it is in the intertidal region as well. As we were walking along the water's edge in Juhu one day, Shaunak noticed an octopus, a small one, around 4 inches long, bobbing along on the surface of

---

* See https://ocean.si.edu/ocean-life/marine-mammals/life-after-whale-whale-falls.

the water. On closer inspection, a scene of the hunt was revealed —
how the octopus had lost its life is anyone's guess, but it proved to be
an opportunity for a lot of creatures. To my horror and fascination
(isn't it always these two when we see a hunt?), I saw that a few of
the octopus's arms were trapped inside an anemone's mouth. The
sea anemone, this sessile creature that looks dainty and pretty like
a flower was devouring an octopus because it came in its food path.
The sea anemone has been known to be an opportunistic feeder
as well, eating what it can even if the size isn't proportional (very
relatable, just so you know). Then along came the hermit crabs and
the nassarius snails for their seats at this table. In the wild, when
an animal loses its life, it becomes a sort of ecosystem for others.

In the terrestrial forests, these form a chain of command —
first the large predators, then the smaller scavengers, then the
avian vultures, the insects, then the bacteria and fungi, and back
to the earth. This occurs in every possible way, nourishing an array
of lives in the process.

What a world.

You met some assassins. Now let's see some defensive
superpowers.

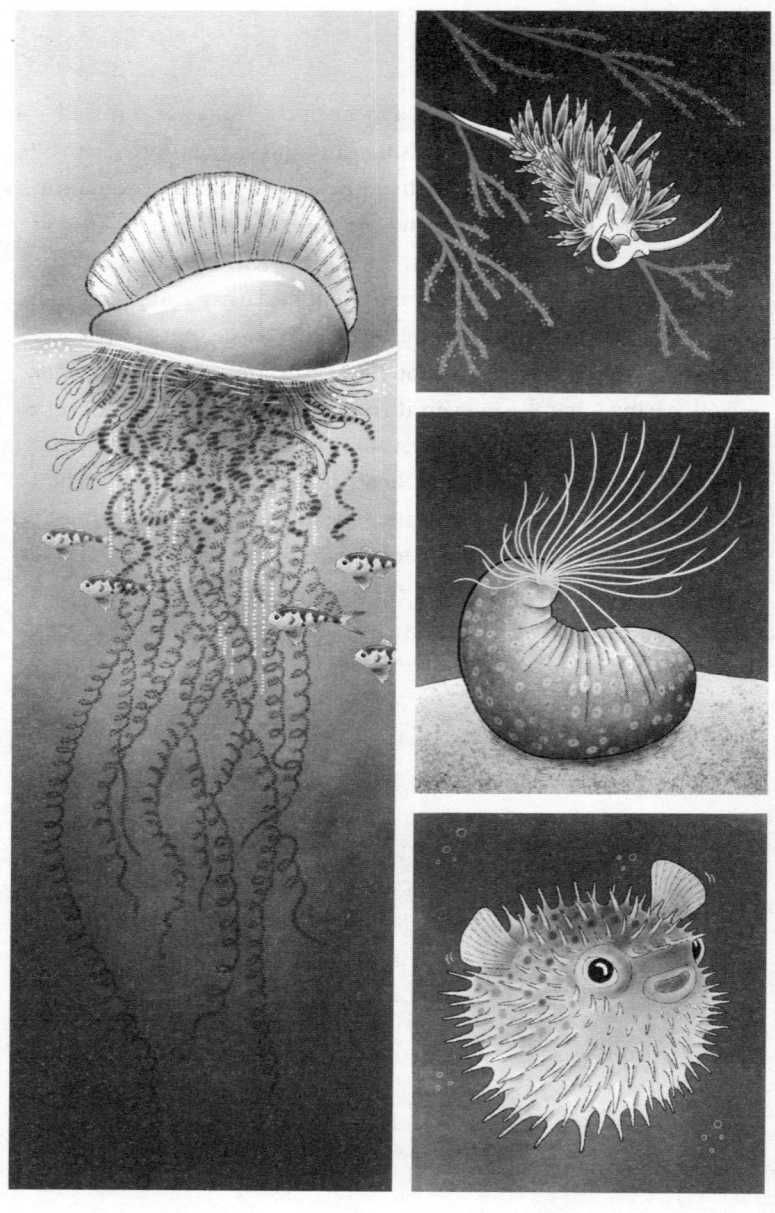

Clockwise from left: Defence mechanisms — the seasonal beauty of the Portuguese Man o' War; the weapon appropriation of Cratena, the gross and effective reaction of a sea cucumber and the ballooning ways of the pufferfish

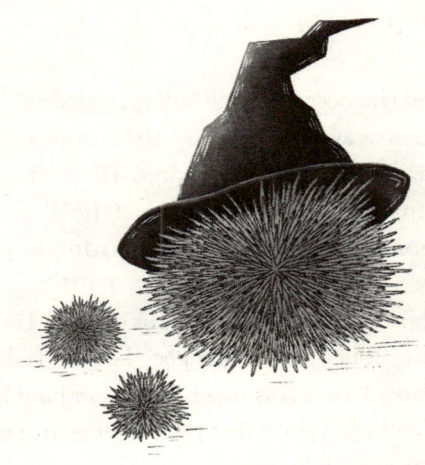

DEFENCE AGAINST THE DARK ARTS*

'*Haath mat lagao, katega* (don't touch it, it'll bite)', he yelled. I looked up to see a man hurrying toward me, a camera slung around his neck and an album in his hand.

I looked back down at the seemingly innocuous creature that would soon become one more reason to love the monsoon. It didn't look like it could do much damage. A 3-inch transparent bubble lay on its side on the brown, wet sand, offsetting the startling blue, purple and pink of its long tentacles. The tide was still a way out, the water far away from this open ocean wanderer. The skies were

---

* 'Defence against the Dark Arts', commonly shortened to D.A.D.A., is the class that teaches students defensive techniques to defend against the Dark Arts, and to be protected from Dark creatures. It is a fictional phrase from the *Harry Potter* books written by J.K. Rowling.

grey and full, and the ocean was turbulent, egged on by the wind. Monsoon was upon us and right on cue, the Portuguese Man o' War (*Physalia sp.*) had sailed onto our shores. The Portuguese Man o' War is a cnidarian. Pronounced 'nid-arian' (the 'c' is silent), these are your sea anemones, corals, zoanthids, hydroids, jellyfish, and all their relatives.

'*Katega ke dankh marega* (will it bite or sting)?' I asked him. He was a tourist photographer. For forty rupees, he would take a picture of you and your companions against the backdrop of Juhu beach, and in twenty minutes, give you a print that you can place in a picture frame at home. In the age of mobile cameras, business is far from booming, but he does get more than a few sentimental, old-school travellers.

He replied, '*Dankh marega* (it'll sting)', kneeling down with me. It was unable to move without water, and only the 'bubble', for lack of a better word, faintly showed signs of life. '*Yeh* waterproof fish *hain* (it's a waterproof fish)', he continued, and said, '*paani ke bahar bhi zinda rehta hain* (it can stay alive even out of water).'

Although he hadn't been stung, he has seen his share of people who had.

'*Sundar hain* (it's beautiful)', I said.

'*Haan, par* danger *bhi* (but dangerous too)', he grinned.

A bit like life, perhaps, I said, and we laughed, watching the absolutely alien creature that comes to our shores every monsoon.

The Art of Defence

Stinging Cells

It's a canteen in the school on the intertidal.

Different animals are eating, discussing their lectures and teachers, and generally bemoaning their lives stuck in school when they could be swimming.

Juvenile damselfish is eating her meal, eyeing the corridor to the deep. 'I want an adventure, like Dory, and here I am learning about water pressure and salinity.'

'You have to understand it though. It's all in the way you navigate water and pressure,' says the pistol shrimp, clicking his powerful claw while devouring his tiny prey.

As the water moves and covers the tide pool, an orange, bright, stem-like being rises out of the tube, like a colourful pencil, up and above until it unfurls like a flower, flashy tentacles collecting particles to feed.

The other filter feeders roll their eyes. 'Such a drama queen, the feather duster worm. Either deep inside his tube or ridiculously over the top. Jeez, there is no in-between.'

Just then, a shadow floats over them. The worm zips back into the tube in a second. The others stop eating. All the groups — the popular sea star table, the studious gastropods, the chattering shrimps, the hard-working crabs — everyone falls silent.

Background score, slow motion. As the cnidarians enter the canteen.

Jellyfish, their tentacles long and swaying, catching the light in a million ways, float towards their table, in that effortless, hypnotic style only the coolest seem to manage, like they've made locomotion an art form. With the rhythmic beat of its pulsating bell, you bet it never makes a bad photo. The long, swirling tentacles gather and unfold like curtains hiding something terrible and glorious all at once.

The Portuguese Man o' War with its violet, blue and pink ringlets reined into an impressive braid nods hello at a small blenny, who immediately blushes and disappears under a rock. Coral colonies, the legit forests of the sea, sit down to eat, nourishing themselves so they can sustain millions of lives.

Closed anemones and zoanthids open up as the water rushes in. They unfurl their tentacles and stretch awake. Zoantharians look around lazily, aware of the effect their stunning blue-green bodies have on others. Their lethal and famous stingers hidden carefully within their tentacles, the cnidarians settle into their tables and silently start to feed.

Slowly, the canteen comes back to life, as the others eat, casting furtive glances at the coolest stingers this side of the intertidal.

~

I'd like you to think of the coolest people you knew back in school. No, not the pretty, popular ones; think of the effortlessly cool, slightly intimidating ones. The ones who didn't need to work for the spotlight because their brilliance just ensured they were constantly in it. Do you remember them? Even if they passed you by with a slight head nod during lunch, you envisaged a wild Bollywood item song in your head. Before we move forward, if you accuse me of playing favourites to this group of animals, you would be correct.

Drum roll

Enter, Cnidaria.

Life out in the deep seas seems other-worldly, filled with wandering creatures with superpowers that are hard to fathom — bioluminescence, advanced sonic capabilities, camouflage, shapeshifting. In that, the Man o' War is a warlord of substantial proportions. It earns its name from its crest — a gas-filled chamber, which looks like a warship floating on the high seas. It uses this transparent bubble, which is anywhere between 4 and 13 centimetres long, filled with part carbon monoxide and part atmospheric gases like oxygen, nitrogen and argon, as a sail to navigate its path on the ocean's surface. Found in the Indian, Pacific and Atlantic oceans, the Man o' War exist in warm, tropical and subtropical waters, and are always on the move. Changing winds and currents push these creatures to our beaches, and you'll see them strewn over the sand, either drying up or waiting it out for the water to carry them back inside. Whenever I imagine the Portuguese Man o' War riding the big wave — and I do for a disproportionate amount of time — the soundtrack in my head is always 'The Winds of Winter', from the sixth season of *Game of Thrones*. Do you hear it? Hundreds of warships powering across the ocean.

The Portuguese Man o' War and the sea anemone make a small cameo in Nick Caruso and Dani Rabaiotti's delightful book, *Does It Fart? The Definitive Field Guide to Animal Flatulence.* Spoiler: they do not. Since the Man o' War is actually a colony of organisms that group together (yes, it's not a single individual, but an army travelling the high seas), it doesn't have an anus or a digestive system. The gassy bit, as the authors say, lies in its chamber. Rebecca Helm is a fellow fan of cnidarian (a group that includes jellyfish, coral, sea anemones, etc.) supremacy (she returned my follow on social media immediately after seeing a painting I'd made of a jellyfish). She said of the Man o' War:

> I love that they have a living sail which is made of actual tissue, like the skin of your hand. It can bend and flex with the wind, and they use their tentacles and their sail to harness air power. They deploy long tentacles to create drag and slow down (like breaks or an anchor) and their sail to speed up! They often dip their sail in the water to wet it and keep their sail tissue happy and healthy!

When you do see them, keep your distance and admire their beauty from afar. The tentacles are packed with venom, and the sting has been described as a red-hot whip.

The cnidarian defence, like most of the powers in this book, isn't targeted at humans. It's not about us at all. The creatures use their weapons against other forces in nature. While they use their stinging cells for hunting as well, their defences are supreme. As Helm says, 'Well, all cnidarians are quite fragile, so when you are fragile, you must be strong in other ways. A sting is a good way to be strong!'

How Does This Sorcery Work?

All cnidarians have stinging cells called cnidocytes, and they use different ways to fire them — harpoon-like structures, sticky substances or even a lasso-like string. All these hold capsules of cnidae, which comes from *knidae*, a Greek word which means 'nettle' — referring to the plant, the stinging nettle. These contain varying abilities and power across the animals, but they all possess them.

The stingers in the Portuguese Man o' War have a hair-like trigger that fires on contact. Therefore, even when it's lying on the beach, stranded and seemingly helpless, it will fire without mercy. Since it has no understanding of your intentions, if you try to pull it off you, it'll continue to fire. An Atlantic counterpart was the largest recorded individual at 50 metres of length! Shaunak has actually found an individual in Mumbai that was 72 inches long. Can you imagine meeting that glorious giant in the water? Good lord, can you imagine meeting two?

Have You Ever Met a Jellyfish?

While they're not strictly intertidal creatures, jellies struck my heart with the force of a thunderbolt. It was at Juhu beach in Mumbai one morning in 2017 that I'd seen one pretending to be a small UFO. It was around 2 feet long, and it lay stranded outside the water, its brown, rust and greenish tentacles gathered and buried underneath the transparent bell. It was obviously dead and I stayed on the shore for a long time, staring at its glistening wobbly surface, wondering where it'd come from and what it had seen. Whether I saw them stranded by the hundreds on a shore in Karwar, or pulsating purposefully in the shallows at Port Blair, I was enthralled by them at first sight.

The Andaman Islands had promised (and delivered) treasures while diving, but I am always amazed by the intertidal zones far more now. The hotel I was staying at in Port Blair had a beach right opposite it, across the busy road. Out of sheer habit, I stepped onto the intertidal zone in the morning, and within minutes, saw a glorious purple bell pulsating in the water by the shore.

Shades of purple and lilac travelled across the bell, which was shaped like a soft crinoline gown, and thick brown tentacles with white tips, no doubt armed with stingers, swam in the water. Helm identified a photo I'd taken and shared that it was probably a species of *Thysanostoma*.

Helm is captivated by jellyfish. She says:

> I am from the desert (Arizona) where water is quite rare. And jellyfish are made mostly of water, so to my young mind, they were very special. I still think this is true, of course. I am a very driven and sometimes anxious person, and jellyfish have taught me that it's ok to calm down, to try and sense and move with the currents of life, rather than fighting against them.

They're also perceived as causing havoc with fishers' catches because of their growing numbers, ringing alarm bells in the fisheries sectors. But there are more than two sides to an overfishing problem. The studies are also diving into the reason of population blooms and climate, so the absolute focus on the jellies' side of it isn't entirely accurate.

I'm often asked why I love these seemingly 'brainless creatures that wander without purpose in the ocean'. It wouldn't be smart to dismiss them as brainless, as so many invertebrates unceremoniously are. Jellies are actually the first creatures that came with an organized nerve net, a blueprint that other creatures used to build more sophisticated nervous systems. I am besotted with a cnidarian's stinging defence: come too close without consent, and you'll regret it. No conversation about what it was wearing (I mean, have you seen a jelly? She dresses for the kill), why she was moving around at that time of the night (it's in the job description!), nothing at all. A potent ZAP, and it's done. And who says that purpose should be what we assign — maybe they're not wanderers, but explorers instead. They might be floating, yes, but it might not be without purpose — they're constantly floating onwards, after all.

Perhaps this could be a lesson in moving on?

Venomous Jaws on the Tips

You met the fashionable sea urchin in the chapter on camouflage. You would think that the spines would be more than enough for this creature's defence; it clumps its spikes together to impale a predator. But here's an added terrifying level of defence: some species have something called pedicellaria, small fleshy appendages with jaws on the tips that bite around to remove dirt and parasites from the urchin's body. This incredibly beautiful creature, about the size of a burger bun, is the toxic flower urchin (*Toxopneustes pileolus*). It has hundreds of these triangular suction cuplike things all over its body—these pedicellariae—and all sea urchins have them. But in the case of the flower urchin, these latch onto anything that touches it (including a careless diver's fingers) and discharges potent venom, in a manner similar to jellyfish stings. The venom is known to cause neurotoxic symptoms as serious as paralysis in humans! However, as with most other dangerous marine animals, this urchin would rather just lie low. It is usually seen slowly ambling across rubble beds. But its cousin—the *Tripneustes gratilla*—is capable of launching a small cloud of detached venomous jaws towards its victim. Each jaw can fasten onto predatory fish and inject it with venom. These animals have no chill. None.

A Puffy Meal with a Side of Poison

Hermit Crab was at her after-school counselling job
She considered the large fish in front of her, sitting, fins drooped
 and listless.
'Let's revisit the incident', she said, as the fish winced.
Hermit Crab ploughed on gently, 'It is, according to me, the root
 of your trust issues.'
The fish lay down on the rocky couch, attempted the difficult
 story.
'It was years ago', he said, slowly.
'Go on', said Hermit Crab encouragingly. 'You were hungry, you
 had said.'
The fish took a deep breath, going back in time.
'I was hungry. I saw a fish in the shallows and made my way to
 it. Easy peasy. I've eaten fish before, just not this kind, you
 know.'

Hermit Crab nods.

'It swims away. I give chase! I reach it, and put my mouth over it . . .'

The fish tears up, and . . .

'Whoop! Its whole body becomes a ball as my mouth is going around it'.

The fish shudders. 'It was two times its size, oh my god.

And it had sharp, poisonous spines!

I was in so much pain! And wrestling with this puffed-up creature. It swam away and I — I was just there, bleeding, in pain and shocked. I don't think I can ever hunt again!'

Hermit Crab made a note and said,

'Perhaps this just means you need to do some homework, perhaps. As we'd discussed before.'

'Ah.' The fish was still lying down. 'I am just so busy in the day.'

Hermit Crab closed her notepad. 'If you'd just make an attempt to know your fish, or even which ones are in season around you in the water, it would solve all your problems.'

'But how can I', he wailed, 'when I can't even trust any?'

Hermit Crab rolled her eyes. Fish could get so dramatic.

~

While most pufferfish are poisonous in varying degrees, certain species of porcupine pufferfish prefer to deploy a two-pronged approach: poison and size. It contains a potent poison called tetrodotoxin, a nerve poison even more potent than cyanide, and far more active than cocaine!

To keep things interesting, research shows that they're attracted to the most toxic partners out of a line-up. Now that's a power couple I would not want to mess with.

These fish are popular with the divers and researchers. They're incredibly curious fish and have often doggedly followed people underwater.

For some species of puffers, a mere 2 milligrams of poison is enough to kill a human being. That makes it more potent than the poison of a black widow spider. There's also a genus, appropriately called *fugu* in Japan, where the most toxic of the species are consumed—it might actually require a superpower to cook, as chefs have to be trained in dealing with the toxic parts. The fish wasn't entirely wrong, Hermit Crab. Sometimes, 'Let's go to dinner' can be a real misadventure.

Chemical Warfare and the Humble Sea Slug

Imagine you are helping a sea slug dress for a night out. Mindful that the intertidal zone is a dangerous place, you'd rather it blends in than stands out. You sift through the clothes rack, looking for something in pastel grey. But when he finally walks out of the dressing room, your jaw drops to the ocean floor. He is dressed for the spotlight in a bright, polka-dotted outfit with an aggressive, rainbow-coloured hemline. His anal gills sit on his back like a small bouquet (some others have hidden gills on the sides), and his mantle edge is fashioned like the hem of a skirt that swirls as he moves along in the shallows.

For a lot of creatures in the water or on land, bright colours usually signal danger. Our nudibranch is warning his predators that his chosen attire isn't all fun and games. Nudibranchs (literally translated as 'naked gills') are sea slugs. They are from the same group as sea snails but have evolved to have no use for the shell and have embraced a life with other means of defence for their soft bodies.

Sea slugs hold a special pride of place in the world of tidepoolers across the world. Shaunak, who has spent years documenting these animals, describes them as 'some of the most diverse, colourful group of creatures. Like in the birding world, they're also a bit of a challenge to spot. Small, sometimes as big as your fingernail, they pose a challenge even to the keenest of eyes—and that's some of the allure. It's like a game, finding and identifying nudibranchs on the shore.' They have these unique colours and shapes, and you find them on specific things in tide pools. That triggered the continuous search for 'nudis' within the group. It spread to tidepoolers across the country and soon, there were chat groups sharing IDs, colours, adaptations, and the oft-abused 'Send nudis' joke.

It was on a shore walk at Haji Ali dargah in 2019 that a group of tidepoolers, including Shaunak and Abhishek, saw an old friend of the city: a small shape on a rock face that didn't look like anything they'd seen before. A white, yellow and pink polka-dotted wonder swirled in the water. A tiny sea slug, 3 centimetres in length, the Bombayana sea slug was publicly recorded in Mumbai after a gap of seventy-two years. It was named after the city and, yes, 'Bombay *ana*' is a very obvious joke, well done you. Although, the joke's actually on us, since scientists are now calling it 'Bombayanus'. There's a joke there that I don't want to make.*

There are many groups of sea slugs, but two of these groups are common and very diverse—dorids and aeolids. Some dorid species wear acidic toxic chemicals like sesquiterpene, which are concentrated along the hem of their skirts, so a bite out of that can prove quite a mouthful for an animal. Other dorids practise

---

* https://www.dnaindia.com/mumbai/report-bombayana-slug-spotted-in-mumbai-after-72-years-2682767.

autotomy like crabs; they voluntarily detach (and then regrow) parts of their bodies, to escape a predator. Yet others have sharp spicules stored in their bodies from sea sponges.

Outside the circle of enthusiasts, not many cared for sea slugs. I didn't either for a long time, at least not until I could spot them myself. But I do remember when a bunch of tidepoolers saw a *Cratena*. Abhishek and Pradip Patade, one of the other founders at Marine Life of Mumbai, were flabbergasted that something this beautiful—that so far they had only seen deep underwater while diving—was gallivanting here, on Mumbai's coast.

But the most interesting superpower of defence is perhaps the one of appropriation.

Let's head for lunch to one of the deeper tide pools. Hydroids grow under the shade of the towering rocks here. This is a cnidarian in possession of some active stingers. In normal circumstances, you wouldn't be able to eat this delectable animal—the orange polyps, juicy as they are, are armed with tentacles and we all know what that means by now.

But your lunch date is the stunning *Cratena*, a nudibranch that has found a way around this hiccup. She looks a bit different than your party partner though.

The *Cratena* is not about the frills and the skirts. She is an aeolid, so instead of the flower bouquet, she possesses cerata, extensions on her back, which give her the appearance of a dragon. These are primarily digestive and defensive extensions, which also happen to be capable of breathing. Dressed in white, with the pink and orange-filled cerata providing that shock of colour, *Cratena* is all understated chic.

Lunch is an exercise in efficiency. *Cratena* moves over to the polyps and uses the dinner process as a sieve. She digests the nutrients from the hydroids and separates the stinging cells from them — it is a bit like sifting the grain across a plate, picking out all the tiny dirt or insects. The orange colour comes from the hydroids it's eating. The orange portion of the cerata is the digestive tract. The nematocysts are only at the tips. They're the white tips we see on the *Cratena*.

Now it has a pile of stinging cells left. But lunch with the *Cratena* is an exercise in zero waste. Instead of throwing this out, she packs them up and stores them in her cerata (now you know where the stunning orange comes from)! She's full from her meal and now has access to her prey's stingers, which she will use to defend herself. It is a bit like if you ate the Bhut Jolokia and then used its most potent ingredients to burn your enemies. At some other lunch date, we will go meet the *Baeolidia* nudibranch, which takes the zooxanthellae from the zoantharian it lives on, and leaves the stingers.

Some chromodorid nudibranchs actually use the legend of the Trojan horse, which allowed the Greeks to get inside the walls of their enemies' city. According to research, by using packaging and offensive weaponry as a defensive variant of the same strategic theme, they 'offer parts of their bodies to the predators, allowing a slightly delayed surprise counterattack in the predator's mouth due to the presence of concealed "gifts". These consist of distasteful compounds delivered at high localized doses that, according to Paracelsus' dose response paradigm, make for a strong chemical defence'.

Lunch, but make it chemical warfare.

Eject First, Talk Later

Sea cucumbers are delightfully bizarre. The name itself tells you how it might appear. Some are genuinely beautiful like the green individual with red spots I saw on the seabed at Havelock, in the Andamans. But most on the shore in Malvan I encountered looked like — and there's no nice way to say this — turds lying in the shallows. This is ironic because most species of sea cucumbers have quite a creative reaction to their predators. If you've ever threatened to throw up at someone as an intimidation technique (yes, I have, so what?) you will appreciate its methods. Unless you're the one doing the threatening, that is.

A sea cucumber will sense danger and upchuck its insides at the predator. But it's not a random projectile that hasn't been thought through. It knows the drill. It throws up an entire cluster of tubes called Cuvierian tubules at the threat. So, if you were too ravenous and in the mood for sea cucumber pie, the determined upchucker par excellence is going to take you on. Like an oddly flatulent Spider-Man, the sea cucumber shoots out tube-like threads from its bum, which could potentially bind the predator — and in some species, these tubes are also toxic.

So, while the human equivalent to extreme danger is — to use the crude phrase — 'crap your pants', which causes zero harm to anyone but you, the sea cucumber has turned vomiting into potential missiles.

In association with the cucumber, to continue this brazenly gross conversation, is the pearl fish. To be fair, the cucumber seems to be an unwilling participant in these goings-on, but here it is. The fish, in a bid to live a sheltered life, will force its way into the body of the sea cucumber — it gets worse — through the poor animal's bum, and lives inside the body, like a squatter who'll never leave. The cucumber will attempt to keep the fish out by closing its anus, but at some point, it needs to open up, for various functions, including using water for breathing, and well, an animal needs to relax at times, even if it is a superhero.

Certain species of sea hares are able to release a type of purple or white ink in the face of an advancing predator. But unlike their fast-swimming counterparts that use this tactic to vanish into the deep blue, these creatures are slow-moving slugs, so at best, this is a sort of defence mechanism aimed at warning the predator to not come any closer.

The cephalopods — octopuses, squids, cuttlefish — famously discharge black ink into the water and use that momentary distraction to propel themselves away from their predators. The moray eel is one of those who gets confused by the smell of the octopus's ink cloud.

The defence employed by the dog whelk (a common seashore snail) actually led to the colour purple's association with royalty. The secretion of a purple pigment to thwart its predators actually flung it from the frying pan into the fire. This was because the ancient Romans and Phoenicians made it into a dye called 'Tyrian purple', which was one of the most expensive commodities of that time. They collected vast numbers of these snails from the Mediterranean Sea, as it took around 12,000 snails to produce a single kilogram of pure dye. With this dye adorning the robes of emperors and kings, purple became the colour of royalty and high status.

Take a moment to imagine a life in perpetual peril. As you eat, sleep and laugh, imagine a real and present demon constantly lurking on the horizon. Imagine knowing that while you doomscroll, or get distracted by a dessert, or just yawn or look away at the horizon, the second you let your guard down, the demon will come get you. We're familiar with fight or flight. In a state of anxiety, or abject fear, our bodies will react to survive. In the wild, in a world full of predators, every animal is given the ability to defend itself. Deer has speed, a porcupine has spines and monkeys can climb trees. Humans have probably been gifted with the ability to think. Our brains prepare how our bodies react under threat. When alarmed (or during exercise), the sympathetic system of our bodies takes over, triggering the fight or flight responses. It pumps blood to the tissues in need, it alerts the body, tensing it for impact, and it prepares us for strenuous physical activity. I'd say a woman's brain might be activating this in various degrees throughout the day.

As the danger passes, the parasympathetic system comes into play. It is responsible for the body's rest and digestion response. It comes into play when the body is relaxed, resting or feeding. It winds us down after a stressful situation and puts the brakes on the pedal activated by the sympathetic system.

On the shore, we see what these animals use — from toxic ceratas and camouflage to stinging tentacles and venom. Here, they assemble with their shields, armour at the ready.

8

TIDE POOLS AND THE CHANGING OF THE GUARD

The ocean retreats deep into herself.

Twice a day, or more, or less. As is her way. Wave by wave, she slowly rolls away, spent perhaps by everything she does at the front lines. As she pulls away from everything she sees, from us, she unveils the shore's secrets, pausing her incessant conversation with it.

She travels to the far recesses of herself for just a few hours, rolling in the deep. Her withdrawal might have killed innumerable lives daily, but she doesn't let that happen. She leaves behind parts of her to hold the fort while she's gone. And so it comes to be that sometimes the size of a cup, sometimes as deep as a small valley, the unassuming tide pool takes charge during the changing of the guard. It provides life to those who need to wait out the tide, and livelihood for those who live by it. For humans and animals, for a precious few hours, it plays the role of thousands of small oceans.

And then, she thunders back in. Powerful, refreshed, the ocean reunites with the starving shore. She pours herself on land, taking over everything she left behind. She fills up the parched intertidal regions, armed with stories and creatures from the deep. If only it were possible to ask a returning tide what she saw, and who she met and what her travels have taught her. How much richer could our lives have been if she could tell us what we won't ever be able to see.

The ocean's depths might terrify us. Now think about what it would mean if the ocean could tell us what the animals think of us when we dive to meet them, what jokes are cracked at our expense when we carry our own canned air or channel our fish suits to match the originals. What do they think of us? Maybe they love our enthusiasm, our curiosity. Maybe they have checklists the way we do. What if, somewhere in the ocean exists a database like *iNaturalist*, where we are categorized and referred to.

Imagine if the tide could tell us what happens after those precious 40 metres (where recreational diving stops), or what unfolds at the plummeting depth of 300 metres (the height of the Eiffel Tower), then lower still at 500 metres. Imagine if she could share with us the stories of the terrifying abyss below 1000 metres, where sunlight no longer reaches.

As Abhishek once said to me, 'Can you fathom, that at depths below 1000 metres, there exists a world that possibly has no idea about the centre of our lives—the sun?' They don't know trees, plants, humans, sunlight or moonlight—nothing at all. What can she tell us about those alien worlds—if we asked her, for example, what lies beneath 1800 m, where valleys and mountains exist (and it is as deep as the deepest point of the Grand Canyon)? What would she tell us about the dark underbelly of the earth where, even if you upturned Mount Everest, there'd still be room to go further below? She could tell you about when Don Walsh and Jacques Piccard went to the depths of 10,994 metres, where no one had gone before. Oh, the stories she could tell us, if she could communicate — of the deep, of distant shores and ancient people, and dormant volcanoes.

For now, the sentinel tide pools willingly vanish into her. They are invisible again, non-existent even, with no form or shape, waiting until she calls on them again. They dissolve into her embrace, no questions asked, knowing full well she'll leave again.

Knowing full well she'll return.

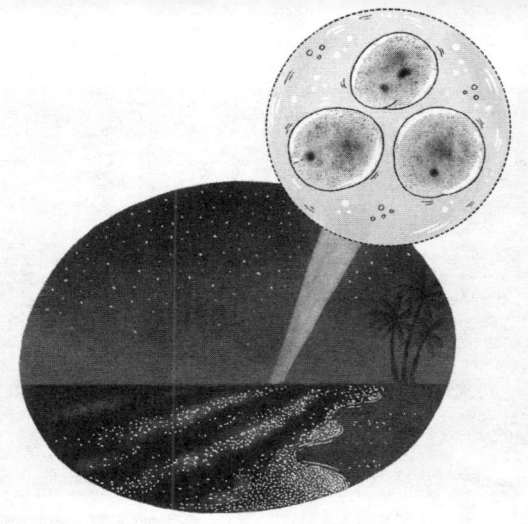

9

WHO FIRED
THE BAT SIGNAL

BIOLUMINESCENCE AND
THE MYSTERY OF
THE GLOWING BEACHES

It's a dark night.
The moon is but a sliver in the night sky
The waves softly rumble as they move back and forth.
Hermit Crab walks along the shore.
There are couples afoot, she notices.
Some hiding in the shadows and some walking hand in hand
*   along the water's edge.*
The beach just somehow calls for romance, doesn't it?

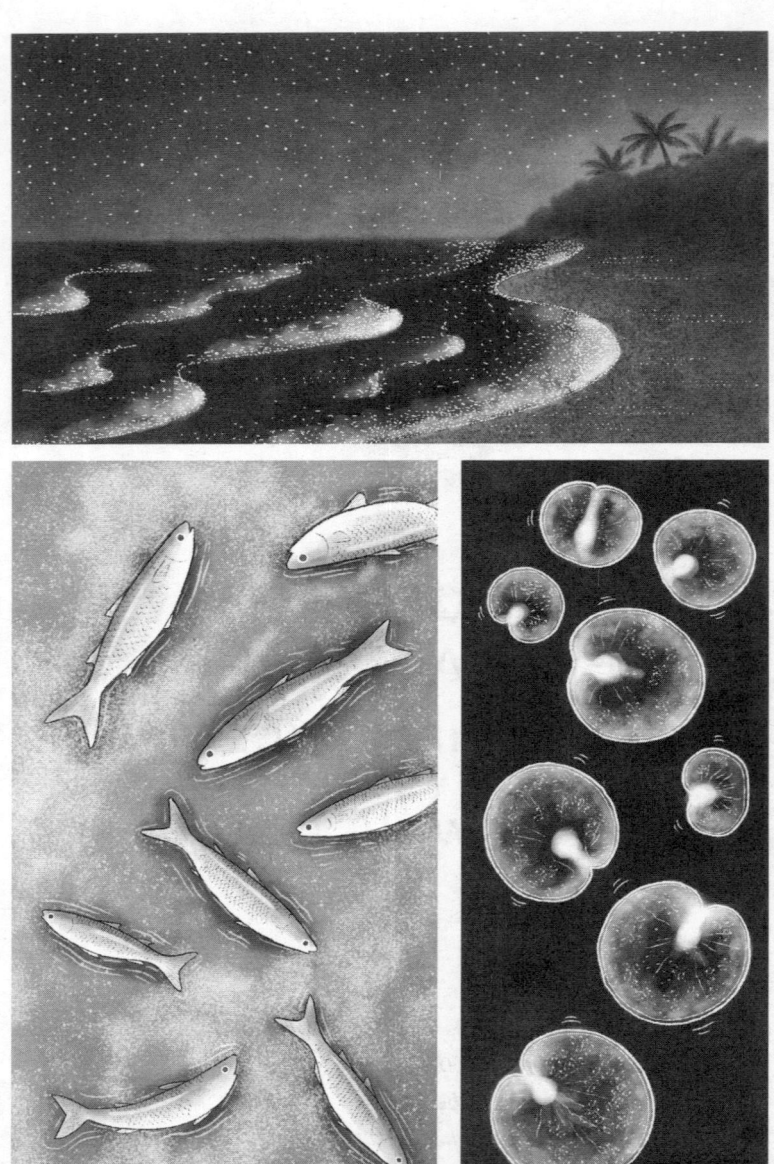

Clockwise from top: A glowing beach; getting up close and personal with the *Noctiluca*; death rises out of the depths

It's the horizon, she thinks. That's what everyone wants the
*   photo for.*
The breeze swirls around her mischievously
And then, as if on cue, the waves start to fire blue sparks
As Hermit Crab watches, the white turns to sparkling blue.
As wave after wave glows up the beach
The humans are positively dizzy with elation,
All rushing to the water, whipping out their phones
Trying to take photos in the dark . . .
Hermit Crab watches in amusement and exasperation,
Careful to stay away from the water.
She watches the screaming humans, so excited about the blue,
Oblivious to the fact that beneath the waves,
Where the beautiful bioluminescence lights up the dark
(and tremendously beautiful it is, she admits),
Dead bodies float to the surface
As the visiting plankton takes life after life.

~

I n the dark of the night, a coastline takes on a new meaning.
    On one such night, with just a sliver of moonlight in the sky,
only an inky black ocean remained. The water seemed opaque, as
if purposefully closing the door on the secrets of its abyss. Kashid
beach is an hour's drive from Alibag town, a popular tourist spot
at any point in time, which became a number one destination
during the pandemic in 2020 – 21. Its proximity to Mumbai in the
face of air travel restrictions enhanced its appeal manyfold.

    It was still evening when we stepped down 7 – 8 feet, from
boulder to boulder, from the road. Despite a not-so-low tide, the
water had retreated more than I'd expected, and large patches of

the rocky platforms jutted out of the wet sand. I expected to be on the beach well beyond nightfall, having come to see a very specific marine creature: a light-bearer plankton — *Noctiluca scintillans*. It was a single-celled organism called dinoflagellate, and was a kind of marine plankton.

A coastal town around 96 kilometres south of Mumbai, Alibag is part of the Mumbai Metropolitan Region. Coastal areas like these are familiar to this little visitor. Earlier in 2021, as the lights went down around Juhu beach, it made the waves glow blue as they crashed on the shore. Different coasts have local names for it; some fishers in Malvan have likened it to *kajva* or fireflies. Marine biologist friends lovingly started calling it *chamki*. You've seen the phenomenon happen in photographs of the sandy beaches in Maldives or other foreign destinations. You know the ones I mean, where the shores look almost fluorescent blue. And while most of the accompanying information is full of romance and beauty (I hate being the harbinger of buzzkill), the plankton is a harbinger of death for everything that lives there.

How does the plankton manage to be a supervillain? It attacks the very core of what animals need to survive — food and oxygen. Mahi Mankeshwar is a marine biologist studying the *Noctiluca* plankton and its effects on the life around it. Her research attempts to discover a possible transition happening at the base of the food web in the Arabian Sea. *Noctiluca scintillans* is native to the Arabian Sea, which is not new. Mankeshwar has seen seasonal blooms of the red *Noctiluca* in various parts of the coastline, especially in south India. But the plankton that animals know and are used to is being replaced by something frightening. While it isn't a plant cell, *Noctiluca* is now using a symbiont that is green, basically carrying a plant cell inside it so it can photosynthesize. It is this combination that gives it the bioluminescence. Mankeshwar said, 'The symbiosis of the old noctiluca and the green members living inside gives it the superpower of being able to thrive in otherwise uninhabitable waters. Even the green type occurred in the Arabian Sea now and then but was never as pervasive as now, possibly due to climate change, and anthropogenic reasons.'

This plankton is not palatable to many otherwise plankton-eating creatures like sardines and mackerel; only jellyfish and salp (a kind of marine animal) seem to be able to feed on it and thrive. In that, it is literally altering the food chain.

I started to check the tide pools. We still had hours to go before nightfall. I am a creature of habit, drawn to patterns that are familiar. My muscle memory understands how to navigate a rocky shore and anticipates what I might find there. For example, at Juhu, I know where the brittle stars chill or where the sea stars might be waiting for the tide to come in. Here I was somehow hit by the unfamiliarity of a familiar space and was quite dazed at Kashid for the first half an hour.

Slowly, the rock pools started to talk back. Ah, there are the shallow algae pools, must be *Elysia hirasei* (a sea slug that feeds on algae) territory, and yes, there was one. The small pops that pistol shrimps make announced their presence. Connections began to form in my mind—creatures and food preferences, safety sites, and so on. The shore map began to unfold in my mind. Hermit crabs, my old friends, scuttled about decked in various homes of different sizes.

'*Noctiluca*', said Abhishek, who'd accompanied me for this trip. He pointed at a tide pool. I gingerly rushed over the wet rocks and peered into the tide pool. Thick, greenish-yellow, swirly ribbon-like formations floated on the surface. I wondered how many times I might have seen this before mistakenly dismissing it for algae or even scum. Within minutes, we were staring at the plankton through a macro lens, and saw clusters of individual round organisms, like light-green microscopic olives. Such a small thing to look at and see the havoc it can cause — a bit like the bringer of the pandemic we've all come to enthusiastically detest.

To some marine ecosystems, *Noctiluca* comes prepared for life as a supervillain. It chokes the life from everything around it. A bloom travelling with the current spreads fast, sucking up all the oxygen from its surroundings. This is bad news for pretty much everything but here's why it is particularly devastating in the Arabian Sea.

One of this sea's features is that it has an oxygen-minimum zone in surface layers around 50–150 metres deep. This means that below the surface, parts of the sea have waters with extremely low levels of oxygen, which is essential for life to thrive. When blooms expand rapidly there, fish die. Two years ago, a strange 'fish die-off' happened in the coastal region of Alibag, Varkala in Kerala and Karwar in Karnataka. Rays, sardines and shrimps literally began to jump out of the water and die gasping at the coast. The scientific community was divided in its opinion. While some cited water temperatures and currents to be possible reasons, others cited the possibility of algal blooms and pollutants to be the causes. If it were indeed the dire effects of *Noctiluca*, that would be what the last stage would look like — where there isn't enough available oxygen for the animals to breathe.

I'd wanted to see the plankton for years, having narrowly missed it every time. I'd been the target of the most unpalatable memes when, after a whole ten months of being in the city, *Noctiluca* came knocking in Mumbai the first night I left. I watched from far away as the marine biologists sent me photos with 'you have to admit, Sej, it's funny! The one night you're not here!' Oh, ha ha. Yes, it's ridiculous, and shut up. I spent the night feeling unreasonably bruised and hurt by plankton that I suspected was deliberately avoiding me.

As the light faded over Kashid, darkness crept over the shore, boulder by boulder. I sat by one of the tide pools, my pants lined with sand. The tide began to turn, like clockwork. The shore was empty, aside from us. In Mumbai, we're not used to two things — seclusion and darkness. No matter what time of night it is, we'll see people out and about, with lights gleaming on the smallest street corners. Our beaches are well lit. Here, far behind us on the hill, our car was no longer visible, cloaked by the night. The lone chai stall had been packed up. The occasional pair of headlights would rush past us but otherwise, the shore was almost devoid of human presence. To me, sometimes, the same spaces that provide escape and comfort during the day seem uncertain and unsafe in darkness.

Bill Bryson, an author everyone must read, wrote in this glorious way about the Appalachian trail:

> Woods are not like any other spaces. To begin with, they are cubic. Their trees surround you, loom over you, press in from all sides. Woods choke off views and leave you muddled and without bearings. They make you feel small and confused and vulnerable, like a small child lost in a crowd of strange legs. Stand in a desert or prairie and you know you are in a big space. Stand in a woods and you only sense it. They are a vast, featureless nowhere. And they are alive.

The shore that night was alive too. Despite the vastness that you can actually see, the ocean and the sky seem to meet, dissolving the horizon into a giant, limitless blackness. The rocky outcrops were now black hillocks with sharp edges, crawling with invisible creatures; you are no longer as sure-footed on the slippery intertidal zone as you were in the day. Night on the intertidal stretch is busy, perhaps twice as much.

Is a beach as different as the colour of the sand? While we wait for the *Noctiluca*, let me take you on a quick detour to Akshi beach in Alibag. On this vast beach, the wayward scrawls the water makes on the sand will tell you how far the tide had reached earlier that day. These patterns become our shore whisperers that tell you about the tides and currents. Akshi's landscape is eccentric — sand banks, the massive rocky patches and then again swathes of sand. It is at these shores that the tide turns dangerously. You don't know how deep it gets, and there's a real danger of drowning. We were there after sundown, and in the distance, on a rocky patch, fishermen collected clams, crabs, oysters and snails.

There are some common, traditional methods of fishing here: '*Haathphera*' — a small net which is dragged by two fishermen, using gill nets, before dol net, hook and line and cast net. Pomfret, golden anchovy, Bombay duck, barramundi, kingfish, Indian salmon, Indian mackerel, mullets and croakers are the popular catch here.

At Akshi, we lost the fisher silhouettes to the night, only the powerful beam of their torches giving us clues about their movement. The sky was starry and it met the horizon in a dazzling display of light and dark. The fisher torches were reflecting off the tide pools and seemed to beam up to the night sky. It looked like the set for *The X-Files*. I would have liked to read lines with Fox Mulder.

But, on the night of the arrival of the *Noctiluca*, Kashid was the beach for the other-worldly. I hugged my knees to my chest and watched the vast expanse of the sea. Stars gleamed in tandem, so many of them that you feel they might fall out of the sky for lack of standing space. The sky was full, enormous and infinite; below, the ocean, with its soft roar, was giving my anxious heart comfort.

As the water flowed in, the plankton began to glimmer, outlining the rocks where they met the incoming rivulets of water. When physically disturbed by the surf, the plankton glows with the help of a photoprotein called luciferase.

Now, while the reaction is due to a mechanical movement, it's not exactly a defence mechanism, contrary to popular belief, and while lighting up, it sends out a flare. Research shows that this becomes a sort of inadvertent defence mechanism against its predators. Larger predators follow the light and come for the jellies or salp feeding on the plankton.

The water lapping the rocks was glowing with a faint blue hue. I idly put my hand in the water shook it. The splashing made the water turn blue. I pulled my hand out and stared at it, which continued to glow in parts, like some kind of tattered glow-in-the-dark glove. Damn, *Noctiluca*.

An hour later, the shoreline was aglow. It started with small flashes of blue streaking across the waves. Then, it transformed into a dull blue. Slowly, as the water rushed in, wave after wave flared up, as the coast continued to throw up a blue glow. I'd never seen anything like this before. We'd obviously unwittingly stumbled on one of the sets of *Avatar*. Now, here's the part that is difficult to confess. While I knew that this was here to snuff out life, I could not help but be moved by the hauntingly beautiful sight of a coast lit up by plankton. The smaller tide pools around us were suddenly flaring up too, and I watched in disbelief as fluorescent shapes — fish, shrimp and crabs — swam and zipped through the pool, coated in the glowing plankton, like my hand had been.

What a deadly beauty this was, and how conflicting the entire moment had been. How could something so glorious to look at be so terrible?

'Bloom proportions have increased', said Mahi. She added:

It's seasonal now, meaning a new normal is forming. We need to study it to understand how animals are adapting to this. Fisher catch will be affected too, the jellies that follow these blooms fill up the nets, and they have no economic value at all. Will we need to plan around these for our fisheries? These are questions we need to answer with data.

The next time you see *Noctiluca*, of course, you will be enchanted by a glowing beach; I was, and will remain so, perhaps. But we can attempt to understand what is happening, at least.

There might be no mal-intent in the natural order of things, but there is death all the same.

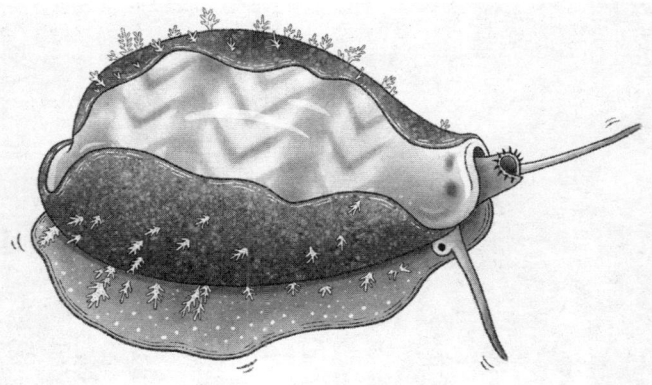

10

THE COAST AS A SHAPESHIFTER

The fishing boat rocks gently on the surface. The blue-green water laps against its hull. The sun's rays glint off the water, creating dancing slivers of light. On the deck, the catch of the day is being sorted, all being prepared to be sold at shore. All, except one.

A large creature breaks away from the sorting hands. As you watch, a bulbous head with long, snaking arms slithers its way along the wooden deck—an alien doppelganger, in some ways. The Pacific octopus reaches the side of the boat in full view, almost in a defiant manner.

You can see that it has no intention of going quietly.

As everyone on the boat watches, the octopus finds a tennis ball-sized hawsehole, squeezes one of its arms right through

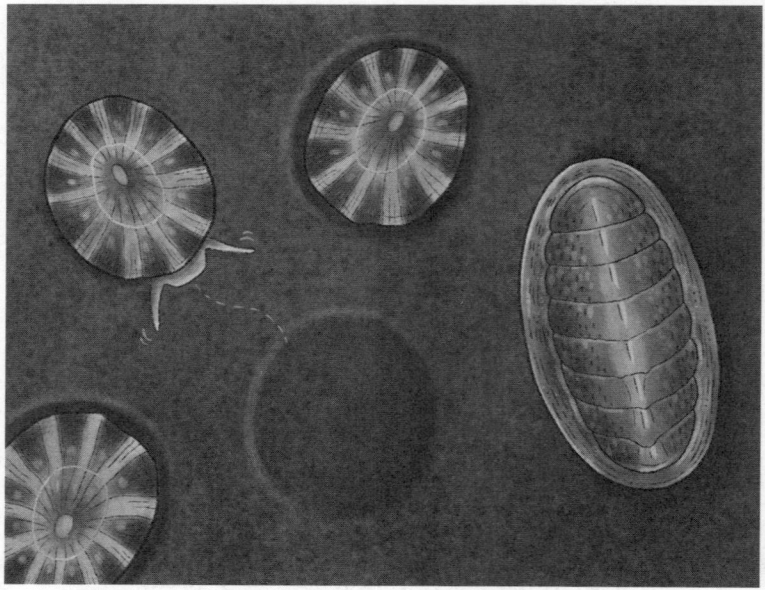

Coasts shapeshift over time, over painstaking processes, and over constant
work. Tiny sculptors like the limpets and chiton help out

it and feels around, lower and lower, until it feels the water's surface almost 2 feet below. The fact that within minutes, it has seen the deck, calculated that the water is accessible through the hole, and managed this escape, means that it has mentally navigated the path to its destination.

Then it does something even more unbelievable.

The 3-foot-long octopus proceeds to squeeze itself through a hole less than even half its size.* Methodically, it shoves itself, arm by arm, finally by its head, appearing to be semi-liquid in the process, until it emerges on the other side and plops down into the ocean.

In pop culture, shapeshifters use their abilities to transform in battle. It's a high-stakes power. Mystique's terrifying yet glorious true self is constantly hidden under different faces and bodies.[†] Loki, appropriately called the 'God of Mischief', could take on animal forms and human forms to hide his true self.[‡] Moony, Wormtail (ugh), Padfoot and Prongs stole our hearts by their animagus abilities, not to mention the firecracker McGonagall, whose watchful black cat avatar started our relationship with the *Potter* universe.

How did the octopus manage to escape? The absence of a hard skeleton allows them to squeeze into crevices literally half their size, making them Houdini-esque escape artists — they have been

---

* See an octopus squeezing into a tube a https://www.youtube.com/watch?v=LNvMgGpGrrs&ab_channel=NationalGeographic.

[†] Mystique is a fictional character from Marvel Comics, commonly in association with the X-Men. Created by artist David Cockrum and writer Chris Claremont, she first appeared in a comic in 1978.

[‡] Loki is a fictional character from Marvel Comics. Created by writer Stan Lee, scripter Larry Lieber and penciller Jack Kirby, 1949.

known to escape aquarium tanks by squeezing into the seawater inlet and travelling down the pipe!

A creature that loved occupying drainage systems was the terrifying Pennywise from Stephen King's *It*, who haunted all our nightmares — a clown who promptly assumed different shapes and realities to pounce on every kid he saw.

The first actual memory I have of being aware of a superpower that allows you to change your body composition was through my first love, Bollywood. Before then, I'd read loads of children's books where gorgeous magical things happened. Children sprouted wings and flew to the clouds in the sky, fairy tales told of curses and boons that facilitated such transformation.

But to see it happen in Bollywood with Sridevi on screen was mind-boggling to me. There had been other instances in the past (and there will be others in the future), but an entire generation of Bollywood audiences were obsessed with Sridevi's transformation into the *ichhadhari nagin*. She did one snake dance in white-clad, silver-eyed rebellion and the rest of us were enthralled. The fact that the movie had three parts and spawned so many television adaptations showed that we just could not get enough. The terrible and overarching effect was the irreparable damage to education about snakes, which generations of researchers are now trying to clean up — much like the negative impact of *Jaws* on sharks.

Anyway, I digress.

In the intertidal zone, animals like the octopus shapeshift in style, within seconds. Animals use many other ways to transform. Certain species of both sea cucumbers and ribbon worms can shift shape from small, stubby-looking blobs to snake-like lengths.

But I'll nudge you towards different manifestations of the same abilities. I'd like you to think about shapeshifting but as a slower transformation, like a coast changing over time. Oceans change over the course of our lives. They shape shores painstakingly slowly, over centuries of wave action, deciding what should remain ours and what they will take away. They perform a distribution of resources in a way. They've taught me that reclamation is not a human prerogative.

Why should we know this, though? It is because we stop noticing the small things when they happen every day. Our bodies are changing every single day, and we won't know how much it changes until we see someone years later and notice the things we would miss if we saw them every day.

Suvrat Kher, a geologist, says,

> Coasts are not static entities . . . Any complacency we might have accrued by watching the same timeline of high and low tides affecting our familiar beach must be tempered by this realization, that our coasts are being re-sculpted continuously. Our cities, our agriculture, our ways of life, that we build along coastlines must adapt to this inevitability.

Coastlines and how they change helps us understand how the places we live in might look in the future, how climate has affected us in the past and it whispers to us what we might need to do to survive.

That's one reason, but also, as Suvrat laughs and asks, 'Who doesn't want to understand how the earth works?' His attitude is entirely on point—geologists are after all historians, building narratives of earth processes. They've gleaned so much of our history by peering keenly at rocks, which are the ultimate archive of the earth's conditions. Geologists like Suvrat are reading the earth through the vastness of time spans—the transient nature of even the most rugged mountains, and the inevitability of catastrophic events shaping the character of our planet. Geologic processes operate on a variety of timescales, from hundreds of millions of years to a few hours. Our future changes too will operate on various scales.

The rock type found on the western coastline in the Mumbai– Konkan area is basalt, same as the rest of the state, and it's about 65 to 66 million years old, 'except in Mumbai, where slightly younger (around 62 million years old) basalts and lava types are found', he points out.

A whole 62 million years young. That sounds about right.

Dr Lalitha Kamath is an associate professor and the Chairperson at the Centre for Urban Policy and Governance, School of Habitat Studies. She worked on a study to explore this question through the experiences of Mumbai's indigenous fishing community, the Kolis, that live amidst the wetness of the Thane Creek, Arabian Sea and Ulhas River and the expanding concrete of Mumbai, Thane and Navi Mumbai.* For all this talk about rising ocean levels, the fishers told her that in some parts, the sea has actually receded a kilometre and a half over the last sixty years. For her study, she conducted a participatory mapping exercise with the fishers to trace the coast and its history. 'When narrating histories, they talked about events', she said, and that 'they would use timelines of cyclones or floods, basically of an event at sea, it's not a linear timeline. Just how fisher time is about tide, and moon cycles, not according to years and hours.' The fishers held memories about the Second World War, where the navy had taken over the jetty and set up a bomb disposal there. They remembered the receding water through these timelines. They tried several

---

* See https://www.inhabitedsea.org/the-sea-and-the-city.

explanations—garbage, pollution and even construction work. Lalitha said:

> They know how things change because they have their ancestral fishing grounds in the sea, called Saj, passed down by generations. They bury bamboo and stakes in the sea, setting a fishing area for each family and one has to abide by the rules of how those stakes were placed. You couldn't block others, and if you didn't fish, you leased it. They talk about it like [a] house in the sea. They use parallels like a farmer too. Like how they'd say 'lands are bad'. That's how we feel sometimes, about our spaces in the sea. Because the water level has reduced as well along with receding coastline.

A number of processes affect coastlines. The rise and fall of the sea level over hundreds to thousands of years will result in landward or seaward shifts in the location of the coast. A cyclone can change things overnight. Kyar, the cyclone that rose from the sea over Maharashtra, played havoc with the coast. Shaunak remembers stepping out on the Malvan beach after being closed in for three days as the storm raged outside to see large swathes of sandy areas where there was water, and vice versa. A small beach shack was floating far off in the water. The coast was unrecognizable.

Do you remember I told you about the limpet and its home scar in 'Chapter 2: A Secret Forest'?

Isn't that also a sign of a changing landscape? Pay attention to it, that small indentation when you next step out onto a shore—it's like the outline of a small vessel carved into a rock. Where did that come from? From a limpet, or a chiton, from years ago.

Umeed Mistry—diver, photographer, film-maker, and an absolute fan of the intertidal zone—has been fascinated with the concept of time and space. Umeed says:

All it has taken is a chiton or a limpet to come and fix itself on this rock. To think, 'I like this place, it has just the right amount of sunlight, moisture, temperature, wave action and salinity. This is fantastic, this will be my space now'. Bit by bit, it wears away that bit of rock and makes a tiny pocket there, a little niche it calls home. Then, you observe that pocket for a timeline that goes over 100–200 years. That animal has long died, and some pieces of gravel have got stuck in that niche, and the waves hit them repeatedly and churn them around like a mixer, where it wears away a larger and larger chunk of rock and creates this beautiful vessel. A small bowl carved into a rock face.

On a walk, when someone comments, 'this is an interesting shape', think about what went into making it, and the way the water is able to do this work over time, all because of its ability to sculpt.

Shapeshifting over time, over painstaking processes, and over constant work.

Like a human being going through life, perhaps.

~

I am going to take this thread and tie it with another, so bear with me here.

The largest shapeshifters are our coastlines; among the smallest, at least among those visible to our eyes, are mantles.

I am an 'omnivert'—as a personality type, I possess both extrovert and introvert behaviours, depending entirely on how

I feel. In a way, I adapt and blend into an appropriate personality around the people that I am spending time with, so much so that the Johari window's exercise once led to an almost existential crisis (it's a technique developed by psychologists to better understand your relationship with yourself and others; how you see yourself and how others see you).

The more I know about the superpowers of the animals of the intertidal zone, the more I have wanted to possess the little hacks that they have evolved with. For example, in an uncomfortable setting, perhaps a cloak that reflects how I feel would be beneficial — perhaps some mood-driven fabric that reveals or hides what I am feeling at the moment, or even better, something that allows me to clamp tight until I feel sociable enough to charm the pants off you.

By definition, a mantle is a cloak. While all molluscs (the larger umbrella term hosts sea snails, sea slugs, limpets, clams and octopuses, to name just a few) have one, what each does with this cloak is up to them.

The planet Earth has a 'mantle' too; it sits between the brittle crust and the dense, burning core of the planet, and it makes up for a whopping 84 per cent of the Earth's volume.* In that big ball of fire, the mantle contributes to some shifts — activity inside it leads to volcanoes, earthquakes and the movement of land mass.

The molluscan mantle is, in comparison, a cloak, a soft covering made of tissue. The mantle's primary function is to hold and protect the internal organs of the mollusc. It's like a backpack with multiple features and it's used in whatever way is best for the animal. For example, the octopus uses its mantle in a spectacular fashion, making invisibility a thing of envy. For some bivalves (a

---

* See https://www.nationalgeographic.org/encyclopedia/mantle/.

clam, oyster or mussel — anything that has two hinged valves that close together) the mantle becomes a part of their siphons, a tube that it uses to sniff around, follow a chemical trail to hunt, or throw out excess water.

Try this: during a walk on the shore, look out for thin jets of water shooting out from under the rocks. It'll likely be more visible on a rocky shore. It'll appear like multiple leaks on a rocky waterbed, water forcefully rocketing out of the earth — and then there will be one more, and one more behind that. Suddenly, it will appear like the whole patch is a miniature version of the Bellagio Fountains (for those in Mumbai, Juhu beach is a good place for this).

Get down on your knees, and when you look a little closer, you'll see a siphon. It is a small, pink fleshy tube that fills up with water (you can see it filling up, a bit like an injection) until it's engorged, and then it ejects a stream of liquid out like a *pichkari*. After this, it becomes flaccid until it fills up again. Yes, I am still talking about the bivalve, get your mind out of the gutter, people. That's probably the *Donax* clam (and lots of other species) and its siphon hard at work.

Then there's the cowrie.

You've met various versions of the cowrie in its afterlife. The shells are used as souvenirs, for the decorative tips of your pants' strings, in the clasps of necklaces, in the bands of your slippers. They're colloquially called *kaudi*. A cowrie's shell has a history in the world's trade industry and was, back in the day, a legitimate form of currency. They came in ships from the Maldives in exchange for cloth and rice, regulated fiercely by the Maldivian King. As early as the eleventh century, the cowrie began its journey across the world. Their association with power and status, as well as the ease of usage, made them a popular form of currency.

There is good reason for that—it's one of the most gorgeous snails on the shore, with one of the shiniest shells you ever saw. If there were an equivalent of a shiny-hair commercial, where a woman walks all over town tossing her hair around to the envy of the balding and oily-haired bystanders, the cowrie's shell was born to play that role.

'Most sea snails have a fleshy "mantle" that is inside the hard shell, encasing the organs and producing the calcium carbonate that makes the shell', said Abhishek. He added that:

> Cowries, however, do more with it. Their unusual mantle can extend sideways and upwards to cover the entire shell, polishing it and keeping it shiny. A cowrie's mantle also has a complex surface—branching protuberances help it to breathe, and the uneven surface helps break its outline for more efficient camouflage. Some species also have mantles that match the colour of their habitat.

Seashells are our most immediate connection to the ocean. I could wager that most of you reading this have strolled down a beach at some point and been wildly delighted by the kaleidoscopic display of seashells scattered all over it. As children, we have carefully collected the best, most colourful ones, engaged in some collector's vanity and even played some games with *kaudi* (small cowries). We've held the conches to our ears and told ourselves that the ocean is whispering to us. In truth, the hollow shape of the conch amplifies ambient sound—the wind and our ear acoustics—which our brain likens to the roar of the sea. Indians have used conches for religious customs, and they are even used in Buddhist rituals.

When you start looking at tide pools, shells are still your first frame of reference. The process of searching for something in a tide pool can seem a bit opaque when you first start, or at least it was like that for me. As a novice, I would peer at what could only be described as a puddle (reminiscent of the ones I see on the roads in the monsoon), with a group of overly excited scientists pointing at various miniscule things.

In that scenario, your eye focuses on shells. Whether they're being used by their original owners or by hermit crabs as second-hand homes, the sight of seashells is comforting and anchors you in familiarity. At a small cove near Majali beach in Karnataka, the entire shore seemed to be covered in shells abandoned by their original owners. We walked on stretches of just shells, all crunching underfoot, our steps hastening their fate of becoming part of the sand.

Let's Consider a Sea Snail That's Making Its Own Shell

One of the most fascinating superpowers of a mantle is its ability to make shells for the animal. Why is this so amazing? When you look at the shell, look at its architecture. Look at those exquisite shapes and sizes, custom-made for the animal's lifestyle.

I was surprised as to how many people who came for shore walks did not know that the sea snail actively makes its own shell. It is not an object that is detachable, nor is it something that it is born with. The shell is a home they construct, and they evolved the tools to do this with — the most vital one being the mantle.

Dr Helen Scales, the author of the wonderfully written *Spirals in Time — The Secret Life and Curious Afterlife of Seashells*, likens it to the art of the ancient practice of coiling pottery. Think of a spiral shell. The mantle starts by secreting protein, then comes a layer of calcium carbonate, created using calcium from the surrounding seawater, and then a layer of smooth nacre to keep the snail's soft body safe. The mantle keeps building this at the outer edge or 'lip' — the part near the opening of a shell. That's how the coil grows, until it becomes a spiral shell.

But the superpower that truly boggled my mind was this: Scales talks in the book about the possibility that the patterns on the shells of these animals are not random; that the molluscs might have the ability to read them, like the pages of a diary. It stems from the fact that since shell-making is time-consuming (and here the transformation process is different from the immediate powers of Mystique), it is done in bursts, over a period of time. In recent studies, scientists have put forward the idea that these patterns might be like bookmarks, to remind the animal where it left off so as to not mess up the geometry. The implications of this idea for an invertebrate are staggering to me.

They come without anything and all, and over time, transform into creatures that have built their armour, their homes, their defences, their retreats, their worlds. The next time we see a shelled creature, we need to remember this. The next time you see a shell that you've put on a shelf in your house, remember this.

It's the memory of the animal.

It's the equivalent of a sea snail carving on a wall somewhere:

I was here.

This is what I saw.

And this is what the ocean was like.

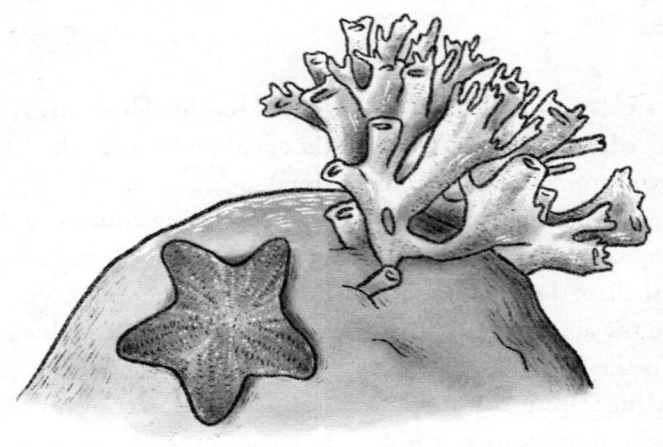

I I

TIDAL PHOENIXES

Superpower: Regeneration

There's a plot point in *Deadpool* where Wade Wilson, played by Ryan Reynolds, is able to showcase his regenerative superpowers.* A mission resulted in both his legs almost being blown off. A memorable, if slightly bizarre scene has him, a grown man, sitting on a sofa, regrowing his legs, which were like those of an infant. His power is to be able to heal from anything. He can take a bullet and he can explode and grow back—his persistent regeneration is a cause of constant annoyance for his enemies.

---

* Deadpool is a fictional character appearing in American comic books published by Marvel Comics. Created by writer Fabian Nicieza and artist/writer Rob Liefeld, 1991. See *Because Science with Kyle Hill*, S1, Episode 72, https://www.youtube.com/watch?v=P1wZ1Hp9eLw&ab_channel=Nerdist.

In Deadpool's case, his disease is the wheels to his powers.

We're obsessed with stories of healing—of bodies, spirits and minds. The proverbial phoenix is a favourite protagonist in fables and folklore and underdog stories. Among vertebrates, this is a far harder feat. While salamanders have very high regenerative capacities, in a study conducted in America, researchers found that some alligators can regrow their tails following partial injury or even substantial loss of the posterior tail segment.

For the superheroes on the shore, cell regeneration happens a bit like the High Priest Imhotep in *The Mummy** or even Claire Bennet from the show *Heroes*.[†] These characters come back from burns, stab wounds, and bone loss; they simply refuse to die from injury.

Human beings don't quite get second chances in the same way, but we know a little something about healing. Reparative regeneration is when our bodies regrow things that we've lost or broken, like tissues, hair, skin and bones. It's common in both vertebrates and invertebrates. The latter just does it better.

I am going to take you through this chapter in a trajectory of different regenerative potentials. First up, we have the creatures that can come back from almost nothing—like worms and sea sponges—followed by creatures that need some important bits to regenerate like the phoenix—for example, sea stars and crabs.

---

* *The Mummy* (Alphaville Films) is a 1999 American action-adventure film written and directed by Stephen Sommers. It is a remake of the 1932 film of the same name.
† *Heroes* is an American superhero drama television series created by Tim Kring that appeared on NBC for four seasons from 25 September 2006 to 8 February 2010.

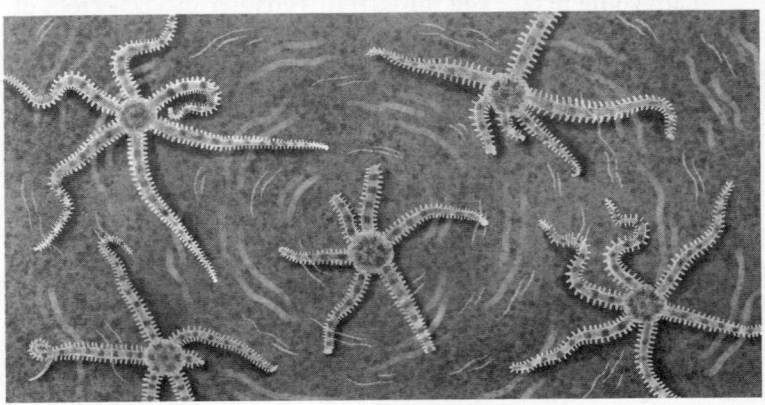

From top: Creatures regenerate in different ways. Sea stars, porcelain crabs and brittle stars heal in varying, astounding degrees

Back from the Ashes: Sea Sponge and the Powers That Be

Stephen Hillenburg, a marine science educator, created the popular series *SpongeBob SquarePants* for Nickelodeon in 1999. It was based on an unpublished book he created called 'The Intertidal Zone'. For show creators inspired by this book, you know where to find me.

There are creatures that regenerate in a way that is truly astounding—they regrow completely even from almost nothing, from the tiniest of pieces. Studies show that sea squirts can regenerate their entire bodies from just a fragment of their blood vessel, due to the presence of stem cells!

When I saw a sea sponge for the first time, it made me curious about the person who'd seen this animal and thought, 'I have found the protagonist for my cartoon show.' A primitive creature, it is often mistaken for a plant, a fungus, or even a non-living object attached to a rocky surface. Some species look like a small cactus, but without the thorns and with pores all over.

Sea sponges are bright spots of colour in contrast to the usual brown and grey of the intertidal zone, dressing up in pinks, blues, yellows and oranges. It is sessile, sometimes flat, sometimes tube-like, sometimes branched, and to add more confusion to the 'is it a plant' mix, I've heard a patch of them referred to as a sponge garden. However, they're very much animals, and one of the earliest ones to have arisen on the earth. The fossil record is rooted in the Cambrian or Ordovician periods (that's around 541 to 444 million years ago). Their cells don't form tissues and organs like most other animals that came after them; rather, they are simply an unspecialized mass of similar cells, hence they are characterized as 'primitive'.

They belong to a phylum called Porifera, which means 'pore-bearing organisms'. If you zoom in with your camera, or through a macro lens, you'll see the minute pores which the animal uses to draw in water currents, to filter-feed on plankton and other organic matter from the water.

Being this simple in form and low on evolution, sea sponges have a powerful capacity to regenerate. Under adverse conditions, sea sponges can literally collapse and disintegrate, leaving behind spherical reduction bodies. When conditions are better, they reassemble to form a new sponge. Remember how that villain comes back together from liquid metal in *Terminator 2*? This is a bit like that. Don't we all know a bit about biding time until it's the moment to roar?

Down the Wormhole

My only interaction with any sort of worm in my life has been the common earthworm, which would wriggle out from the earth by the hundreds during the monsoons. And while those held their own abilities, marine worms possess powers beyond reasonable belief. I was late to this party, far more enamoured by the camouflaging octopus and the tentacled jelly. Worms seemed so very commonplace, until they didn't. They're up here with the sea sponge because they too can reconstruct themselves into full creatures from almost nothing.

At Dana Pani, in Madh Island, Mumbai, I came across a strange little creature. At first, I thought I'd imagined it. The tide was rolling in, and as the water flowed over a small patch, I thought I saw a flash of orange, but as I looked closer, it wasn't there anymore. Dismissing it as a trick of the light, I sat down next to the pool, tired from the harsh sun. Sure enough, there it was again — a small orange flower swaying in the water. The feather duster worm, from the genus *Sabellidae*, is what you'd call a bit of a drama queen.

Hiding when its tube is exposed to the air, you won't see the animal, but you'll spot just the tube. When submerged, the worm comes out to feed — and here's where it unfurls its flamboyant self. A bright, stem-like being rises out of the tube, like a colourful pencil, up and above until it blossoms open like a flower, generating a water current to breathe and collecting particles to feed. The minute it senses your shadow, it zips back into the tube in a second.

A whole bunch of them can do magnificent things, but nothing quite as dramatic as regeneration. Reshma Pitale and Sudhanshu Dixit are two of the few researchers working on a species of worm called flatworms (you met them in the reproduction chapter, the penis duel-happy bunch). In India, Sudhanshu Dixit, a project scientist at the Centre for Marine Living Resources and Ecology in Kochi, has described thirteen species, seven from the Andamans and five from Lakshadweep.

Both of them agree that little work has been done on these creatures, which makes their efforts challenging and thrilling. Out of the 1010–1015 species of flatworms identified by science, only sixty-eight are from India. Sudhanshu says: 'It's tough to work on them. They're small, and tough to spot and even more difficult to preserve as they're such soft bodied animals.' But they're still working on it, passionately spending their days on shores, looking under rocks and beseeching flatworms to show themselves.

Largely all marine worms regenerate, but in varying degrees. Some species of flatworms have been known to grow back after being cut up into pieces in labs. Usually, the rule for the polyclad flatworm is that regeneration of all its cut-up parts (including the eyes) is possible if the brain remains intact.

It was on a walk at Malvan, Maharashtra that Shaunak documented a perplexing sight. He was peering around in knee-deep waters of the rocky shore for intertidal creatures, and came across a worm that was an absolute beauty. Marine worms are startling in colour—this one was 4 inches long and its body was orange and white with black dots around its edges and a beige middle with scale-like patterns. It looked like a small, long dragon fruit, or a certain big cat. The tiger flatworm (*Maritigrella makranica*) might have been disturbed by the activity in the water, and he saw it tearing itself lengthwise. It is likely that both parts became a separate animal. Abhishek has seen these on dives, describing them as 'a glorious flatworm from our west coast reefs. *Maritigrella* roughly translates to "little tiger from the sea". And "*makranica*" refers to the Makran coast of Iran, from where it was described'.

There are the wonderful polychaete worms or bristle worms. They're called so because they have protrusions on their bodies (chaetae), which are made of chitin. Some species of these look like the worms we're used to, except for their colours—like the pink rag worm or the regal bottle-green paddle worm. Both of these belong to the Errantia. There are others, like the Sedenteria, which largely live in tubes. These are extremely interesting creatures. Polychaetes readily regenerate missing or damaged parts—even heads removed by predators are soon replaced. This sort of behaviour is more common in burrowers and tube dwellers. Some species from the genus *Dodecaceria* can regenerate their entire body from a single segment!

In marine animals, asexual reproduction and regeneration often, but not always, lie on the same page. Remember the sea anemone that fissioned into two in the reproduction chapter?

Splitting into two happens in some polychaetes as well.

The ribbon worm with the scary proboscis from the 'Assassins' chapter belongs to the group called Nemertea. These regenerate readily and reproduce both sexually and asexually, so basically splitting into two happens especially when irritated. B.F. Chhapgar wrote that 'it can be cut up into a hundred pieces, each of which will grow into a complete worm, provided each piece is more than half as long as its body width'.

New research hastens to let us know that this is not a blanket rule for this phylum. Of the 1,200 known species of Nemertea, regeneration has been described in just a few, and none has been as championed as *Lineus sanguineus*: 'Individuals of this species can be repeatedly amputated until the resulting worms that regenerate are just 1/200000th of the volume of the original individual. Furthermore, a complete animal can regenerate not only from a thin transverse slice of the body, but even from just one *quadrant* of a thin slice.'

~

The press conference is about to begin.

Hermit Crab, new-shelled and dressed up for the event announces:

'We're gathered here today to felicitate the team that helped stop the inter-pool gang wars that had caused nothing but havoc for all of us. As you all know, it wasn't even safe to venture out alone'.

Damselfish mum in the crowd says to her friends about her baby damsels: 'What a nightmare, I had to come drop and pick up these juvies every tide in the middle of a workday.'

The others nod sagely but are keener to get a glimpse of the sea star.

The sea slug continues: 'The echinoderm team, we thank you for your service. Now calling the favourite of well, everyone, the sea star.'

Wild applause as the sea star takes the stage and the mic.

'Thank you, thank you.

First, let me apologize for being late. But I was finishing the publicity tours for my new book and motion picture. They just announced it last month, I am sure you saw it all over the news. And you know how children adore me and I had to stay for photos and autographs.'

Crowd sighs.

'It was a team effort, as you can see two of my arms are now growing back.'

Crowd ooohs and aaahs.

'The brittle star lost some limbs too but she's fine as you can see.

The urchin stabbed so many of the enemy, they left with some of her spines still in them.'

Crowd yells and stomps as both wave and blush.

'And the sea cucumber, man, that guy. He literally just upchucked his insides at them, grossed them out and is now regrowing it all.'

Sea cucumber waves awkwardly, not really one to like the spotlight.

'What a crazy bunch. We couldn't have done it without your support. Keep helping us keep our intertidal free of crime. Good day and good luck.'

Crowd goes wild as they wave and exit the stage.

~

There's an interesting group of animals you'll meet during a shore walk—echinoderms. The term means 'spiny skin'. You'll most often have a chance to meet and greet these four echinoderms—sea stars, brittle stars, sea cucumbers and sea urchins.

Sea stars (starfish) have been stars in our bedtime stories for as long as we can remember. As children, that's the shape we associate with constantly shining stars — for good homework, a star atop a Christmas tree, 'Twinkle Twinkle Little Star' and whatnot. That shape triggers nostalgia and delight. When you see your first sea star (and this has been evidenced through four years of taking people to the shore), which is albeit tiny and often hidden under a coat of silt, you'll feel that childlike delight again. They look like they literally fell out of the sky.

Sea stars can grow into an entire new sea star from just a severed arm, provided some of the tissue from the central disc remains.

Unlike sea stars, which use a sort of internal hydraulic system to move with their tube feet, brittle stars can use their five snaky, slender arms (up to 60 centimetres in some species) for movement. Think of Mr Tickle from the *Mr. Men* series but with five arms, all of which can grow back if it loses any of them. However, only the sea star can grow into a full animal from an arm.

The central disc is patterned, and the animal often looks like a long-petalled flower. Since these arms are flexible, brittle stars are the speediest of all echinoderms as they grab, pull and row their way across the intertidal zone. This is quite helpful, as they have numerous predators, so they take shelter under rocks during the day and are largely nocturnal. The slow-moving sea star, on the other hand, will still be hugging the rock with its hundreds of feet even if you stopped the walk for a tea break. Many species of crabs and lobsters, including the porcelain crab, an absolute pink beauty on a rocky shore, can regrow their limbs after shedding them. The porcelain crab gets its name from how brittle it is — it breaks its limbs quite easily.

While all these echinoderms can regenerate, they do so in varying degrees. These animals can regrow their arms, guts, spines and feet, and they sometimes also use this power for reproduction.

Empowering Others to 'Phoenix' as Well

You met the sea cucumber in the 'Defence' chapter—it throws out its insides and repairs them. Incidentally, sea cucumbers are adding their muscle to the regeneration of ocean life as well.

A rather perplexing headline I came across in February this year told me that sea cucumbers can poop over 60,000 tonnes of sediment across a coral reef each year! According to the co-author and marine scientist at the University of Newcastle, Dr Vincent Raoult, 'It's approximately the mass of five Eiffel towers.' Despite the reef being crapped upon with five times the mass of a 'poopular' tourist destination (okay, sorry), this is apparently good for the health of the reef.

Immensely tickled by the sheer irony of the animal's own resemblance to human poop, I went on to read that this process, 'called "bioturbation", plays an important role in coral reefs by aerating the sea floor, providing "fresh" sediment, and releasing calcium carbonate into the water as a by-product to help support coral growth'. Helping regenerate its surroundings—good cucumber, that.

While reading for this chapter, I was pushed to think about our capacities for regeneration. While they're not as impressive as that of these animals, they *are* marvellous, aren't they? The way our bodies heal after disaster hits them is such a powerful thought.

Our resilience, determination and sometimes the absolute lack of choice pushes us to get up every time we are knocked down.

As humans, we know how to heal from disaster. Our physical bodies yes, but even our minds possess the capacity to heal.

We are familiar with catastrophes. Just like the flatworm, survival comes to the front lines and lays out the blueprint for healing, while we fight it out in the trenches.

Yes, we know how to deal with the big things.

Our entire being comes to fight. We fail, we fight. We fall, we get up.

The human mind and body know how to rise from the ashes.

In fact, in body and spirit, what stumps us, are the paper cuts, the smaller hurts. We hardly ever do anything for them. They're not big enough to worry about, but they're there, hurting every day. They fester until they become big wounds.

And then you have the same road map to healing all over again.

Even in our minds, it's a bit like that. We know how to deal with irreversible loss, death and the big things.

It's the smaller tectonic shifts in our lives that we cannot understand. Falling out with family, a lost friendship, a toxic workplace, or apathy toward the elderly—these daily rejections fester. Perhaps in our hunt for powers, we might earn value from fixing the smaller leaks. Fix an arm, perhaps—or even fix that scratch on it.

Focus on the healing. Look to the sea sponges, the brittle stars, the crabs.

Instead of being a superhero who never bleeds, perhaps we can learn how to heal.

SURVIVALISTS
ON THE SHORE

If my life were portrayed in a superhero comic book, the opening panel would be hyper colourful. Head girl at a college, captain of the sports team, gorgeous hair as wild and free as a horse's mane, powerful, popular, loved. Spotlit in a sea of students.

Now zoom into the background. See that girl tripping over her own feet with food in both her hands? That'd be me.

I have lived among enough superwomen and supermen to know that the one superpower I possess is that of survival. Which is not a light superpower by any means, if you think about it. Humans do this well, with far fewer powers than their shore counterparts. The animals in this chapter have different degrees of a solid Plan B either with inbuilt weapons or resilience and improvisation. Most intertidal life forms are well-adapted to living here, but some use their adaptations in extraordinary ways. In a world that's scary and full of things that might hurt them, they make their way. Like some of us.

Let's go see.

Plan B

The *Elysia sp.* and Its Chlorophyll Hit: A Solar-Powered Slug

Hermit Crab and Nassa Mud Snail take a stroll along the neighbourhood.

Mornings along the tide pools were busy.

Hermit Crab liked walking around. It was like reading the newspaper.

She could know what was happening in the tide pools.

They spot a group of Elysia sea slugs and sigh: Oh dear, not this again.

The Elysia are all standing under sunbeams, apparently in some kind of a trance.

Hermit Crab and Nassa Mud Snail make to leave without being spotted, but it's tough to run with a gastropod.

One of the sea slugs spots them.

'Friends, come do some surya namaskars with us.'

Hermit Crab flashes a grin. 'We're fine, thanks.'

'Come now, the sun is the giver of all life.

It allows us all to make our food if we let it.'

Hermit Crab is quick to correct him, 'Um no, it allows you to make your food because you have the photosynthesis tools.'

'Oh, that's just detail. You have to believe. Tell me, do you believe?'

Hermit Crab and Nassa Mud Snail shake their heads and leave to find algae.

From top left: Sun worship with the *Elysia sp.*; the OG swag of the horseshoe crab; and the famous fish out of water, mudskippers

'Hipsterism always comes with a healthy dose of privilege, no?'
They chuckle and move on, leaving the Elysia bowing reverentially
to the sunbeam.

~

I am going to take you to see *Elysia hirasei*, but please be forewarned that when I first saw this sea slug, I was enormously underwhelmed.

The shore near Haji Ali dargah itself is a challenge, which is always interesting. Slip here, and the barnacles and oysters, thousands of them lining the rocks, will slice up your skin. This shore prompted the inclusion of first-aid kits on shore walks after assorted people whooped and landed on their bums, reaching out with hands and legs for balance, only to meet the sharp edges of these dwellers. In all the years I've driven past the famous dargah, I never realized that this kind of wealth lay in its backyard.

Across many tide cycles, we've been there at the shore after the morning call to prayer, as the walkway gates opened up and the morning was still dark enough for the mosque's lights to remain switched on.

We've stood in awe, the sea around us, high-rises not yet awake, the sun beginning to rise, with the city's famous backdrop. In that brief calm, Mumbai is stretching awake, gorgeous, unguarded and still. Later still, as the prayers are done, people spill onto the shore, for a few minutes of silence, love and communing with the breaking ocean before reality hits.

That morning, though, there was suddenly a fair bit of excitement among the tidepoolers because of the *Elysia hirasei*. I squinted purposefully at the foot-long tide pool everyone was crouched over.

Nothing.

The tidepoolers around me were in throes of slug-induced delight, shouting 'OMG, LOOK AT IT!' And I remember thinking to myself, 'Yes, very nice, I'd love to, but where is it?'

First, it was the size of a fingernail clipping. Second, Pradip had to place a ten-rupee coin next to it, just so I could spot it. I saw it at last, a tiny green being foraging for algae. It looked like a floating piece of debris if I hadn't peered at it with my nose almost touching the water in the pool. I blinked, and suddenly I couldn't see it anymore.

I picked myself up, brushed off the dirt from my pants and walked away to other pools to see (hopefully) larger creatures. I made a mental note to tell the team to add creature sizes to their social media posts. With the highly magnified images they put up, people would come expecting slugs the size of plates or something.

Over time, I was introduced to its powers. There are animals on the shore that have a plan B to survive in case they don't get their food. The *Elysia hirasei*, like some other creatures, usually feeds on algae. You'll see rhinophores — the slug's smelling organs — stick out like bull horns, and when you watch an *Elysia* chomp its way across the algae of the intertidal region, you'll be strongly reminded of a cow munching on grass in a meadow. Now, in the absence of that, it can feed on green algae without digesting the chloroplasts — the cell components that let plants photosynthesize — so it can utilize them for itself.

Do you see what it can do? It is able to perform photosynthesis, the way plants can, using the sun. It can make its own food in the presence of sunlight, using stolen equipment. A sort of solar-powered sea slug, this.

And readers, the next time I was not quite so disrespectful, despite the fact that more than a few cousins of the *Elysia* use this tool to make food. Additionally, look close enough (preferably with a zoom lens), and you'll see how beautiful it is. There's a spot of red on its head, if you're looking for a tip to find it. In fact, it became something of a challenge to spot these on shore walks. In Goa, where a dedicated community of tidepoolers thrives, Danika Tavora and Abhishek devised an actual game called 'Spot the Hirasei'. It resulted in a tiny huddle peering helplessly at algae pools for this creature. But make a game, and sure enough, someone will create a hack. Soon, people started bringing magnifying glasses to try to spot it.

You Scratch My Back . . . Shore Partnerships

We're geared towards mutualism, commensalism and even parasitism, depending on the role you play, and your idea of belonging. The second wave of the COVID-19 pandemic hit us with a fury that destroyed lives. We lost people by the lakhs, to the disease, to hunger, to grief. During this time, while the news was hellfire and death, social media sparkled with the kindness of strangers. People who'd never met, and would perhaps never meet under usual circumstances, helped patients get beds, meals and other essentials. Human beings are known to be compassionate, altruistic even, during times of crisis. Research has shown that if we recognize positive interactions in intertidal communities specifically, it would be significant in understanding population and community in physically stressful habitats. They see it as a long-suspected linkage between biodiversity and community stability. A bit like humans, I think.

During the pandemic, a news story on Koli women talked about solidarity networks in a deeply patriarchal set-up, where rights were practically invisible. They spoke about shielding each other from abusive husbands, lifting the other during financial hits, making *kadak* chai when spirits were down and, despite internal differences, the will to stand strong for the community.

In the intertidal zone, while the motives and drivers are of course different, partnerships save lives. Some species of boxer crabs (belonging to the genera *Lybia* and *Polydectus*) are known to carry sea anemones in their claws as a form of defence. The stingers in the sea anemone's tentacles deter predators and allow the crab to mop up food, and, in turn, the anemone acquires mobility to get access to more food. In this partnership, however, researchers found a surprising consequence. When one of the anemones was taken away from the crab, it split the remaining anemone into two, forcing in a way, asexual reproduction so it'd have one in each claw.

Anemones seem to mingle more than others. Carpet anemones provide shelter to clownfish (remember Nemo?). The clownfish get some prime real estate, with special security fitted in via cnidarian stinger cells — and the fish keeps the anemone clean by eating its poop and possibly smaller animals that might harm the anemone.

Sometimes, a housing situation requires a flatmate. Abhishek was diving at Netrani Island for a biodiversity survey. There were many burrows on the sandy seabed, each with a largish goby fish (a little over half a foot long) that darted in when he came close while swimming steadily along the survey line. He decided to slow down and hover for a while over one of the burrows, and noticed a second creature that was slightly smaller. However, this creature wasn't as alert as the goby waiting nearby. It was slowly moving in and out of the mouth of the burrow. Certain pistol shrimps have been found living in a mutually beneficial relationship with certain kinds of goby fish. A study examined the association from the Indo–Pacific region and found that the shrimp maintains a burrow while the goby (which has the better eyesight of the two) stands guard and warns the shrimp of any danger, quickly retreating into the burrow when trouble approaches. Jamalabad said:

> It was what I had expected from what I'd read before, a kind of pistol shrimp, ferrying sand and rubble out of the burrow, dumping it near the mouth. I was sure the goby was watching me, but the shrimp seemed totally oblivious, just doing its housekeeping routine. Avoiding any sudden movements, I managed to record this on video without startling the goby, which would otherwise have dashed inside along with its busy housemate. The video still serves as one of the best slides in my presentations when I'm introducing kids to the intricate, complex lives of sea creatures.

We've seen many species of gobies and of burrowing pistol shrimp in the intertidal region, but I am yet to see this partnership in this zone.

Living Fossils

Imagine a world millions of years in the future, where everything is different. Climate has changed, people have changed, technology has changed — literally everything you know about the planet has changed.

Except you. You've remained the way you are — and, by some miracle, you're surviving.

That's the horseshoe crab.

Have you ever seen one? It looks its age. An ancient creature, it looks like a hard, unturned bowl with a jagged back and a long spine sticking out from behind. Two Indian species live here: *Carcinoscorpius rotundicauda* (30 centimetres) and the

Tachypleus gigas. However complicated their names are, what is clear is that they look exactly like a round tank.

The coastline in Odisha is unique. Researchers Sumer Rao and Samyukta Rao have been working on documenting horseshoe crabs for two years. 'It's shallow and there's sand through and through. So much so that you could walk 5 kilometres into the ocean and still be 10 feet in water', said Sumer. The intertidal region that they work on is large — almost a 4-kilometre stretch.

Horseshoe crabs look like they have a hard shield on their bodies, and it's so solid you don't think about what's under it. It's when you look on the underside that the ancient and perhaps alien references make sense. They're all claws and look like a giant spider. Samyukta remembers the first time she saw it; she laughed and said, 'They could appear creepy to some people. I was thinking of the movie *Alien* when I saw them, when they move their claws, you feel like something crawling at the back of your neck.'

Due to their appearance, locals sometimes associate them with bad luck. Sumer recounted that:

> This woman from the village was collecting and fishing for prawns. She stepped on one and rushed to the village shaman to save herself. She was confident that if it hadn't been for the shaman's intervention, she'd have lost her leg.

Okay, that escalated really fast. To me, it seems astounding that this creature which surfaced in the Cambrian era — which was 450 million years ago — is relatively unchanged. Add to this list, the nautilus, which started to evolve during the Cambrian period and to some degree, crocodiles. I use the word 'relatively' with purpose, as there is a branch of science that feels that the popular usage of the term 'living fossils' has got absolutely out of hand.

In an article titled 'The Rise and Fall of the Living Fossil' in *Nautilus* magazine (yes, the irony), Ferris Jabr speaks to palaeontologists about the phrase originally coined by Charles Darwin (who did admit that it was 'fanciful but poetic and memorable'). The piece strongly states: 'There is no such thing as a living fossil. It's true that the living descendants of early animal lineages can teach us about their ancestors, but the idea that any species alive today has stopped evolving is simply false. In the last 10 years, scientists have liberated numerous species from this evolutionary straitjacket, including coelacanths, horseshoe crabs, cycads, lizard-like tuataras, and tadpole shrimp.' Nothing stays the same, despite initial appearances.

Fish Out of Water: Breathing on Land

A group of fish is playing tag.
Damsel, Guitarfish and Clownfish have formed a chain and are
   chasing the blenny.
It is one-sided, but then
They are swimming with one of the quickest movers in the
   tide pools.
The chase is intense.
Blenny zigzags between the rocks, wriggles through crevices
   and almost bumps into an older slow-moving limpet, who
   swears at the racket
The tide pool seems too small, they're all swimming with all
   their might,
They've almost got him.
Suddenly Blenny rises up, up, up like a plane taking flight and
   catapults through the surface of the water, straight on to a
   rock outside, landing unceremoniously on Hermit Crab

Hermit Crab shrieks in shock at the wide-eyed Blenny.

*'You gave me a fright, you wicked boy', Hermit Crab whacks a
suitably sheepish Blenny.*

*'I am sorry, I am sorry, they almost got me', he gasped, catching
his breath.*

*Hermit Crab looks into the tide pool to see three extremely
annoyed fish staring up at them.*

*'Blenny, you cannot flout the norms!' yells Clownfish, 'of the
game AND of fish respiratory systems. Get back here now!'*

Hermit Crab grins at Blenny; he's one of her students in school.

'You're cheating, clearly. Get back inside!'

*Blenny settles down on the rock, blowing raspberries at the fish
in the tide pool.*

The fish swim away, grumbling 'Damn show-off, that one.'

~

The tide was still turning. The rock was around half a foot long, and on top of it I saw what can only be described as a fish basking in the sun. Of course, it was not doing that, but there it sat, very much alive, no thrashing around breathless or anything — just a slender, brown-grey fish, contemplating life and its meaning outside the water.

You will see these fish zipping across tide pools on most shores. They belong to an order called Blenniiformes, with 900 species described within it. These remarkable fish are adapting to life on the intertidal in a way that earns them a special mention in this list. Scientists have suggested that blennies leaped out of the water to avoid being eaten by predators. But incredibly, a study shows that blennies have *increased* their intertidal activity — and their time outside the water — to remain above predators that come in with the high tide.

And if that wasn't just powerful enough, this bit gave me goosebumps. The lead author of the study, Terry Ord, is an evolutionary ecologist from the University of New South Wales, in Sydney, Australia. He doesn't think that this is just a survival technique, like mountain lions and bears scrambling up trees when they sense danger. He thinks, and of course this is just a hypothesis, that blennies are 'in the process of moving out of the sea and colonising land on a more permanent basis'.

To seal their ideas of colonization, research also shows that blennies are highly territorial and sometimes remain holed up in crevices above water at low tide to guard their territories. They are both curious and territorial creatures, like goby fish. On a beach in Morjim, Abhishek and I spent a good hour with a blenny that was determined to engage with us. The minute one of us put our finger in the tide pool, it would know about it and come to inspect it, sometimes brushing past the finger, or signalling to it and sometimes even biting it. They have adapted to breathing air using their oesophagus. It's true; some creatures will really do anything for new housing.

For another fish who breathes on land, meet the mudskipper. How does it breathe outside water? They carry air and water by the mouthful when they're out on the shore—a dense network of blood vessels absorbs oxygen from it.

Their bodies are designed to facilitate movement on land: the ventral fins (on the underside of the fish) are fused together to form a cup, which act like a sucker and help the fish to hold on tightly to rocks, wood and other solid surfaces, and the pectoral fins (on the 'shoulders') help facilitate its impressive and athletic hop, skip, and jump routine. Combine this with their ever-watchful, bulging eyes placed at the top of their heads, and they are completely equipped to get away from almost all of your photographing attempts. As I said, it hardly falls in line with how fish ought to behave.

Mudskippers are bizarre to watch, because they slide, hop, and zigzag about on land, unlike other fish. But what I love most about it is where it's usually found. I am going to take you to the mangroves. Wear your squelch-proof shoes, we're off to the mud flats.

Warriors — the Mangrove Ecosystem and the First Line of Defence

It doesn't seem real, this space.

The slush grabs your shoes, and you sink in little by little, as you plow forward. A network of roots spreads out below the surface, as vast as the canopies. Some of them are like arrows, some like giant pencils, and they all rise out of the ground — they are aerial roots that form the most identifiable characteristic of a mangrove forest. These roots venture deep underground and hold the soil, like a claw, solid and unshakeable. They are roots that power a soil system and also help to balance the atmosphere.

Everything about a mangrove says, 'Don't worry we're here, we're rooted.'

These are also intertidal areas, where land and sea meet.

For coastal landscapes, the muddy intertidal with its mangroves form the peripheries of our consciousness. They are squelchy, muddy and slushy, but also drop-dead gorgeous. You can spot a cluster of trees, squatting in the muck, seeming to hold hands at the edge of the ocean, staying close together. They form one silent barrier, acting for the land and sea together, holding a feast for the animals that depend on the ecosystem.

On the Front Lines

The habitat of a mangrove forest is tough. The quality of the soil, the salinity of the water and the tidal action make it inhabitable for anything else but these trees. That itself is awe-inspiring. We tend to think of mangroves as one homogenous group. But if we look closer, there are around thirty-seven species of mangroves in India, from towering trees that grow up to 40 – 50 feet, to squatting ones we see around estuaries — and each adapts to its habitat in a unique way.

How do these mangroves adapt to the salinity? They are the only trees to be able to do this. It stands to reason that they have a coping mechanism. As Dr Sheetal Pachpande, who works with Maharashtra's Mangrove Foundation, says, imagine if you drank gallons and gallons of salt. You'll vomit it right out. Certain mangrove species drink saline water directly, but they need to remove it as well. *Avicennia* (the one with the pencil-like ariel roots) and *Aegiceras corniculatum* have specialized salt glands, through which this concentrated salt water comes out. When that water evaporates, you can see salt crystals on the leaves, which are the most purified form of salt.

Where these species grow obviously depends on the conditions in the area: the salinity of the water, the composition of the soil, what height the habitat is at, and what the freshwater influence is on them. All of this plays an important role. For example, the east coast of India has a large number of mangrove patches because the rivers all flow into the sea, forming massive deltas. That coast has several amazing deltaic mangroves where they're able to spread their root systems across flat grounds.

In Maharashtra on the other hand, the Western Ghats have ensured that there are elevations and depressions, so while the numbers of mangroves are lower compared to the eastern coast, the diversity is still high because different species grow in these areas.

The more famous role mangroves play is that of a 'warrior system' — protecting the land from tsunamis, floods and the onslaught of the ocean on the land. Mangroves are the only warriors who can stand guard constantly. They're land builders — they literally hold the sediment together. Their root system is connected, they stand close to each other so they also form a physical barrier, and in doing so, the wave action is reduced. We have seen the effects of flooding across the world and more so in India. Imagine if we had to manage without even these surviving patches. Not only do they take the hit, sometimes they are even destroyed in the process. Cyclones wreck our shorelines, and we probably should be thinking not just of protection, but also restoration and care of these protectors. Look at the way waste collects here — they're keepers of the evidence of what we do to our oceans, aren't they? Mangrove patches in polluted regions are full of trash, wrapped around the roots, hanging from the shorter trees, stuck in the mud. We throw so much into the ocean and it comes back to suffocate our warriors. While policies and corporations hold a larger key to this, we do have some responsibilities towards these amazing places. Do small things — carry cloth bags, carry your own bottles, and before you buy anything on a whim, ask yourself, 'Do I need this?' These are not hard tasks to accomplish, but collectively, it helps our warriors breathe better.

What Does It Mean When Mangroves Are Carbon Sinks?

We all have carbon inside us, obviously. Plants (and some marine creatures) have a special capacity for photosynthesis. We know that they take carbon dioxide from the air and throw out oxygen. This is done by all plants.

But here's where the mangrove's superpowers help us. The texture of the soil in the mangrove ecosystem is like clay, and sometimes even sandy. In coastal areas, the carbon is first stored in the biomass of the plant (this just means the leaves, stems, roots). Second, it is stored, in a way trapped, in the sediment.

Let's take a mind-blowing detour for a second — bear with me. The sediment in the mangroves that you see is the result of painstaking labour over years. One centimetre of the sediment there takes ten years to form. Which is around 1–8 millimetres annually. The tidal action on our coasts ensures that the process is this slow. Look at the hard work these trees put in.

Back to the carbon: along with the plants, carbon is trapped in the sediment, and due to the make-up of this space, it's difficult for the carbon to escape. Through this, they stabilize the atmosphere. Mangroves have *four times* the capacity to sequester carbon. When the water recedes, the animals of the intertidal region come to the fore. One species of mud lobster was described in research from Mumbai and the west coast in the 1960s. They are nocturnal, and it's tough to actually see one in its habitat. Because of its scorpion-like appearance, locals are afraid of it (in Marathi, it's called *paanbicchoo* — 'water scorpion'), so they won't eat it here, as opposed to Southeast Asia where it is a delicacy. The mud lobster plays an important role in the mangrove ecosystem. It burrows 9–12 feet below the ground. Over this process, it brings carbon from the soil below up to the surface, and feeds on the leaf litter, thus facilitating a cycle of carbon. Crabs perform a similar function, except they don't dig that deep.

Dr Pachpande has extensively studied carbon sinks in Maharashtra. 'Mangroves in just 1 hectare of the Thane Creek were able to sequester 34 tonnes of carbon', she says. Imagine the significance of keeping a potent greenhouse gas inside them. 'This is also why we must think deeply about their protection', said Pachpande, adding that 'if we lose them, they become the source of carbon. When they are cut, or burnt, the carbon stored inside goes back out and increases the temperature and affects the atmosphere. We don't want that.'

No, we don't.

13

SUPERPOWERS AND YOU

She digs the sand out, her little fingers hard at work.
The sand is wet, she packs mound after mound, forming a little
> *hillock district.*
A hermit crab sits at a distance. They look at each other.
She's not afraid of it. She waves at the tiny, shelled creature.
She looks at me. It waved back, she says. The crab.
I indulge her imagination. Okay, baby.
(Little do I know, though.)
I ask her, what does she like about the ocean?
It's big, she says.
That it is.
We pat the hillocks down   She begins to make roads that connect
> *them all.*

What do you like about the ocean, she asks me.

I like that it's always here. It seems very brave to me. Nothing seems to stop it.

She considers this. She goes back to her thought.

I like that it takes care of everything.

Who does it take care of?

All the fish and other things, people, us. Even the sun. It swallows the sun every night.

The sun isn't really going into the ocean, baby. It's actually the earth moving.

She thinks about this a bit. She doesn't understand it.

I let it go for now.

What else?

It doesn't end.

How do you mean?

It just becomes another ocean. It doesn't end.

I am stunned by her reply.

You're right. It goes on. Whatever happens, whatever it meets, whatever form it chooses to take.

It goes on.

Humans have been trying to harness some of nature's powers forever — sometimes successfully and sometimes unsuccessfully — using biomimicry. For example, the razor-sharp efficiency of a peregrine falcon has inspired a military aircraft; the success of the falcon is of course far superior to anything we've ever built. The art of nature-based ambush is popular in the army — using a fan hunt that lionesses use, the art of formations based on tortoises (like in the manoeuvres of the Romans in the Asterix comics, which is albeit not so flattering), the pincer movement, or pack patterns based on the silent hunts of the wolves. Similarly, scientists too have been attempting to help us become invisible using the cephalopod's methods.

We might crave the camouflage of a cephalopod, or the absolute defences of a jellyfish, but if we look at our own bodies and minds, we might realize that we possess immense powers.

If you observe a Sally Lightfoot crab sitting on the lower rocks of the shore, closest to the churning sea, you'll notice how it manages to withstand the constant battering of the waves. There is a moment when the waves are poised to crash over the rock, when the crab flattens and positions itself just right, using its pointed legs to cling on while the onslaught washes over it and recedes. It stays put — most of the time, at least.

The point is, the crab does not attempt to sprint away like a brittle star, or swim away with the speed of an octopus, or even scuttle away hurriedly as you would imagine most crabs to. It knows it will not survive if it does so. A tiger does not attempt to hunt with the speed of a cheetah; instead, it has to use ambush and stealth. A deer does not choose to fight a lion, when it is equipped to run. A bear does not simply be up and about through an entire frozen winter like a snow leopard, just as the snow leopard in the same mountains cannot hope to load itself up on nutrients to sleep it off like the bear. They will fail, and perish.

This is probably nature's strongest lesson to us: we all have our arsenals; it's only a matter of recognizing what those contain instead of aping another's. As humans, we are so distracted at all times that we've forgotten what and where our arsenals are.

During the initial days of my tidepooling journey, I would look at the shore life and wonder:

What is it about you?

An anemone that a group is crowded around, its tentacles spread out, glistening in the sun, as it works on moving things to the mouth at the centre of its disc-like upper face; or tiny Nassa sea snails hunting a sea snake; or a sea star hugging a rock . . . I wonder . . .

What is it about you?

You're tiny. You are almost alien to us, our paths cross only when we venture into your home. What is it about you that has prompted people worldwide to sit and peer into crevices and tide pools? What is it about you that binds this varied group of people together across the world, and closer home? People who had never met each other before, who had very little in common, who'd perhaps only seen a beach at high tide; people who came from diverse backgrounds — be it a writer, artist, student, scientist or a business owner; people from other countries even, who would immediately hit 'follow' after seeing a photo of a tide pool on a social media profile.

And yet, I am not sure, what is it about you?

The first few times I walked with the team, I would step back and watch them. These people, who had never given a moment's thought to tides before this, had now set their monthly plans to them. They all had apps that told them what the water level would be on a given day. Who does that? These people, who had fallen on the treacherous rocks so often, now carried along first-aid kits for newcomers. They would catch trains and buses or drive for hours to reach shores at the most inconvenient times (inconvenient to humans, convenient for looking into tide pools). It could be at 12 a.m., 3 a.m., 2 p.m. or 9 p.m. — it didn't matter. They planned their work and social calendars around it.

'Tide week' became sacred and non-negotiable.

The group shared hot tea and coffee, and brought biscuits for longer walks.

They laughed when they had to wade through sewage to see an animal the size of their fingernail. They discussed shore shoes and quick drying clothes. They helped each other take photos and they warned each other about the terrible effects of salty sea spray on lenses.

Conversations on the beach ranged from the latest OTT shows to the identification of a bivalve. FOMO hit in the form of phone messages to different groups asking '*Kya dikha, aaj kya dikha*' (what did you see today?), the equivalent of a safari in the forest being, 'Tiger *dikha*?' If you ever meet Pradip, who pretty much everyone associated with the coast knows of, ask to see his beautiful album of photographs from the last twenty years of walking along the intertidal zones. In this time of digital photos and hard drives, you would be lucky if he agreed to show you the treasure trove his physical album is.

When Marine Life of Mumbai came into being, the crew that came to help build it was as diverse as could be. Some had nothing to do with science or wildlife or the sea. The ideas and opinions that came in were loud, different and often clashed, but it formed a foundation that understood the power of inclusivity. It helped spread science beyond the boundaries of 'wildlife folks'. It was only because the team was so diverse internally that the communication was far-reaching and magnificent. An artist and marine biologist, Gaurav Patil worked with the Mangrove Foundation to paint and put up posters and guidelines and warnings on Mumbai's beaches for the Portuguese Man o' War in the monsoon. Over the next few years, he went on to make spectacular art about shore creatures for some effective outreach. Sarang Naik has won awards and grants here and abroad with his photographs of coastal life. That's some real-time impact for you. As for Jessica—well, she's made the illustrations in this book, hasn't she?

The shore has built a community of enthusiasts. When you find a tribe, the powers come with it. These need not be the ones you think you're taking back, but the ones that you know only later.

While everyone went their way and the group splintered as voluntary groups tend to do, everyone went carrying a piece of the shore in their hearts.

I wondered about all this while I watched the ocean's retreat, the sun setting the sky ablaze over the horizon, the breeze that ruffled our hair comfortingly, and the animals that lived a life of constant impermanence — right here, where the land meets the sea.

Even now, after each shore walk, people sit around small tide pools and talk about the city, about their work, about the animals they met. As life continues in those mini forests, we discuss our histories and our surroundings. Sometimes, it turns to how many different ways there are to understand your backyard — through cycling groups, heritage walks, livelihoods, geology, marine animals. Sometimes, new participants will vigorously argue about the identity of some animals, and one will reference a book on shells they've recently bought, as the more seasoned ones watch with almost parental pride. Everything is feeding into your arsenal when you understand where you live. What happens when something endures is community. Partnerships make us better. Isolation leaves us empty.

What is it about you that you have forever changed the lives of these people?

Of course, we could first attempt to find our roots in science, and there is actually evidence to derive for our love for all things intertidal. Research has found tidepooling to evoke interest because of the diversity of creatures, and the site itself, the oceanfront.

When you start looking at smaller creatures, you become more interested in the health of a habitat, and not just a single individual.

This way, you ensure your neighbourhood breathes better. Priya Sule, an educator who runs The Owl House, a school for people with special needs, said to me in an interview, 'Changes need to happen close to home. The more you can transact within your zip code, the healthier your most immediate community.' What is truly sustainable is understanding where you live, and what supports it.

But also, sometimes some things are just beautiful, and accessible. There are no answers to why some of us are hooked for life, while others interact only marginally. Love has always told us more about ourselves than the objects of our affection. Our love merely makes them more visible—not just to us, but to others as well.

When I now walk the shores with first-timers, and see their unfamiliarity with the landscape, I realize how sure-footed I've become, how I unthinkingly avoid barnacle cuts, how I position my feet on slippery rocks, how nimbly I am able to navigate the tide that flows back so very quickly.

Vardhan Patankar, a marine biologist who has explored the marine realm for two decades, has pinpointed where this lies. He understands now that the intertidal zone has a certain rhythm. The breaking of the waves, the movements of the fiddler crab, the dramatic turn of the tide—it's so full of rhythm. He said, 'Humans are also rhythmic. But if we can find a way to match ours to nature, we'll find balance.' To me, one of the biggest revelations of the book has been the lyrical prose scientists use when they speak of their subjects, completely debunking the myth of the inexpressive scientist. Every single person who spoke to me (and there were some who didn't) was unabashedly in love with the natural world and showed it.

I've been following Martin Stevens' work on social media platforms for a few years. A Professor of Sensory and Evolutionary

Ecology in Cornwall, he posts about his tidepooling journey with so much wonder that it brings the Cornish coast alive. He said:

> One of the things that strikes me all the time is the diversity of habitats around. Near the rocky shore there can be colourful green and red weeds and sandy patches, and a short distance away large areas of kelp forest or seagrass. Each is so different and beautiful, and home to quite distinct species at times. One of the other things I noticed, perhaps more this year than ever, is how seasonal the marine world is here — many people don't appreciate how much the habitats change underwater as the seasons move on, and how much the creatures vary.

This sort of exploration demands our attention, that we notice things, that we stay present, and make the connections that our privilege allows.

What are your powers? How can you access your arsenal?

Is knowledge your power?

Are you shelled like a gastropod?

Do you have stingers in your arsenal?

How do you deal with situations? Do you stay and fight or do you withdraw?

What is your reactive power?

For example, humour is largely unique to humans. The ability to laugh at things is the biggest superpower in my arsenal. It's how we see the universe around us, which is just a giant opportunity for us to see the other side of things. We lose this ability over time. A podcast called *Hidden Brain* with Shankar Vedant and behavioural scientist Jennifer Aakar talked about the 'humour cliff' poll conducted by the polling company Gallup.

Something was happening to men and women around the world starting at age twenty-three. We stop smiling and laughing. Gallup asked people in 166 countries the simple question: Did you smile or laugh yesterday? After twenty-three, the answer becomes no. And we don't start laughing until we are seventy or eighty. Put differently, the average four-year-old laughs 300 times a day, while it takes the average forty-year-old two and a half months to laugh the same amount. That is what we call a global humour cliff. Our ability to perceive humour drops after this.

Part of the reason coincides with people entering the workforce, where you have to be serious. I think over time, you would like to be taken seriously, and you lose the ability to see the bizarre or the funny side of things.

The shore, the ocean with its vast ability to comfort has made me unclench, breathe and allow for silliness. When my niece Meera came to the shore with me, we found a fun way to remember the animals she saw. She was just beginning to enjoy the *Harry Potter* books and we turned the names of all the animals we saw into spells. At some point in the walk, I asked her to tell Abhishek, who was leading it, what snail I was pointing at. She waved an imaginary wand at him, and cried, 'NASSARIUS!' We giggled, we jumped into the water, we pushed each other into it, we made and destroyed sand mountains, and we lay in the sand and laughed. Humour allows us to come closest to our most authentic self.

The intertidal region allows us a glimpse into what might lie beyond the fringes of our consciousness—what happens in the deep where only our imaginations can work. The water doesn't have boundaries. The coast, the shallows, the deep—some animals commute distances we aren't yet even aware of, going back and forth from the shore to the sea.

Our shores have seen a lot, in the form of infrastructure projects, sewage, oil spills, tar balls, and our constant apathy. The intertidal zones of so many shores in the future could be unrecognizable. Vardhan spoke about the idea of a universe: 'The Fiddler crab taught me that the burrow is its universe, the same way my home is mine'. This applies to any creature that lives in nature, on a coast, and we thoughtlessly destroy so many universes in fell swoops, merely because we don't know enough about them. All the trash we throw, everything we vomit up with our excesses of consumption, goes to our shores. New research cautions against the threat of marine debris on our coasts, and the effect it has on the entire ecosystem. There was once a 6 by 7-foot mattress that washed ashore while I was walking by. What is happening, what are we doing to the waters? While we organize cleanliness drives for our beaches, which we must, we need to realize that heroism is also to see the waste that's being collected and recognize how much of it comes from our own homes. The way ahead is consuming less, perhaps.

According to a piece in Mongabay India about the latest report by the Intergovernmental Panel on Climate Change (IPCC),

The IPCC report concludes that the global mean sea levels will continue to rise over the 21st century, even in the lowest emissions scenarios because of the warming of the ocean, as well as the melting of ice sheets and glaciers. For India, which has a coastline of over 7,500 kilometres, this will mean a significant threat to those living in areas vulnerable to the impacts of sea level rise. For instance, across six Indian port cities—Chennai, Kochi, Kolkata, Mumbai, Surat and Visakhapatnam—28.6 million people could be exposed to coastal flooding if sea levels rise by 50 centimetres and the assets exposed to flooding will be worth about USD 4 trillion.

Countries are experimenting with ecologically sensitive ideas — like a mix of wood, stone and concrete for buildings instead of just concrete, or coastal projects with eco-concrete that have shown positive effects (albeit short-term).* What happens over time remains to be seen but it would seem that the way forward is development that involves the futures of both, humans and wildlife.

Lalitha, whom you met in the 'Survivalist' chapter, considers what the coast and her time with the fishers is teaching her. The fishers know the sea intimately; even the way they looked at time and space was from their relationship with it. They would not talk about distance, but time. How much time would it take to go somewhere depended on what boat it was: *engine wali hodi* (a boat with an engine) or one without. When reading maps, time and depth becomes important. Lalitha said:

> It's a different knowledge system, based on practice, like an ecological sensing. The kind of knowledge that is a. developed by being involved in one's habitat; b. is developed collectively; and c. can be passed down as well (like an apprentice) and is learnt through experience.

And experience is about change. You learn a skill, pass it down, and then it gets adapted to a new generation, a new world. Here, with the changes in tide, fishing and climate, the learning *has*

---

* See https://www.bbc.com/future/article/20200811-the-eco-friendly-alternatives-to-ocean-concrete.

to change. It can't be static. If that didn't happen, you couldn't survive. Lalitha added:

> This ecological sensing has been my biggest learning. I've thought so much more about knowledge and how we transfer it, the politics of it. It has made me think closely about the idea of an expert. Who is an expert? I would lay far more value on experiential expertise, because it's relevant for so many spheres of life. Interaction with environment is how we learn to do things. Our cities are so much about this — they're about networks, about *jugad*.

And the ocean teaches us as well. We learn to listen between the roars the ocean makes — when it thunders, when it retreats, the multitudes it carries, the things it's seen, the adventures it has had. We are without pretence here. How can we pretend in front of something so vast that swallows the earth? How can we strut fake confidence in front of something that has changed the face of this planet? How can we lie to something that has seen it all?

So we don't. And we're finally closer to our true selves every time we meet it at this stretch between land and sea.

We're closest to who we are, or who we want to become.

And then there's the tide.

Observe how it behaves. How it flows, ebbs, allows us in and chases us out.

The eternal secret keeper, the tide. It listens to all of us who seek it out — the triumphant, the heartbroken, the angry, the lonely, the old, the anxious and the delighted. It listens without judgement as we pour our secrets out weeping, brought to our knees. It listens, punctuating our sobs with its soft roars. It takes everything with it, swallowing our lives into its vastness. Lost, it is scattered into a million small secrets, taking it to different shores, hoping to provide comfort to others.

Healing is about moving on, and the shore knows something of second chances and devoting more attention to ourselves.

The tide comes in, and returns with a clean slate. As humans whose life cycles are a map of errors and regrets, would we like the opportunity to live through our days again and again? Ah, but then what about the memories, the joys, the victories? We spend so much of our lives in fear—attitudes shaped by trauma, loss, broken relationships and decisions that failed. The tide simply takes it down and starts over. What a lesson that is. What a visual. What a constant cycle of hope, and yet impermanence. Hala Alyan, in her poem 'Spoiler' writes:

> It might not happen for a long time,
> but one day you run your fingers through the sand again, scoop
>   a fistful out,
> and pat it into a new floor. You can believe in anything, so why
>   not believe
> this will last? The seashell rafter like eyes in the gloaming.
> I'm here to tell you the tide will never stop coming in.
> I'm here to tell you whatever you build will be ruined, so make
>   it beautiful.

Make it beautiful.

The beach then presents us with a metaphor for our minds. We've seen the tide turn differently on different shores. Sometimes, you're complacent in the knowledge that the tide has turned, but it's still in your line of sight, and you'll move back before it gets too close. Oh, but look behind, look how it has already flowed in from the sides, quietly, reaching further and further, until there is a chasm of water between you and the shore, and now you have to swim, wade or tread a treacherous and sometimes dangerous path back to terra firma. In some parts of Malvan, the topography of the sand is such that the water is split into two by a massive sandbank jutting outwards from the beach, so the tide comes in from different directions and confuses you. Navigation on foot is a tricky matter.

The tide teaches you to take the trouble to know it. These are wild spaces, it tells you, and don't take them for granted.

The tide is solid, it is fluid and it is reliable.

When faced with obstacles, it moves between rocks, it slides between crevices, it makes it way. It moulds the shores with this very action, and changes landscapes over time.

It makes its way.

They say go with the flow.

And you know what?

Maybe that's not half bad advice.

The coast, our arsenals and our allies

LETTERS

Dear readers, after reading about these wonderful creatures, I thought it might be a good idea to broach the subject for an actual superhero team — a shore squad, if you will. Ever since I read *The Day the Crayons Quit* by Oliver Jeffers, I was inspired to get some of the shore life to write you all an application to be included in this democratic team. And you might be one of the members of the selection committee for me. So, please give these letters your utmost consideration. Thank you.

APPLICATION FROM CONE SNAIL

To
The Democratic People of the Marine Realm
Ref: Application for team member of the Shore Superhero team.
Dear Madam, Sir,

I am a cone snail.

I am not really one to talk about my powers; that sort of chest thumping just seems bizarre, but I realize that is the format I am to adhere to for this communication.

You might already know that I am one of the most venomous creatures on the shore, with no known antidote. My venom is so toxic, that it pretty much paralyses whatever I shoot, and well, that's the end of a highly one-sided battle. But that is not enough in combat. I train regularly to ensure that my harpoon seldom wavers, and neither does my schedule.

I realize this is a team you are building and I'd like to tell you right here and now, I haven't really worked that way before. I have always preferred to work alone, as most of my former contractors have needed to be discreet.

I do have a professional network though—I know a guy. I have always tidily delivered every single assignment I've ever had before the scheduled time. You will find—in this week—three references mailed to you, sealed and confidential, just for your eyes. Do destroy them afterwards, failing which my former employers will be only too well placed to do it for you. They're all very powerful, you see.

I know that my venom is already under study at your science institutions, and you're trying to see how to use it more efficiently in your medical journeys. In a way, we're already working together, aren't we? I spend hours in the lab myself, and am constantly experimenting with my venom so this would be a good collaboration. There have been a few run-ins between your people and my kind. Unfortunate deaths on both sides, but there are some in your species who are foolish enough to wrestle with us for our shells (the arrogance of the human race to own everything they find beautiful is just startling), and our snails had to defend themselves, didn't they? It wasn't personal. It is also a waste of a carefully designed missile, isn't it? What are we going to do with a giant human? Nothing. I reckon nassarius might have had a go at it had it not been removed, I don't know. They'll eat anything.

Anyway, that shouldn't interfere with your decision. That is all water under the bridge now.

I am also largely nocturnal so I possess the vital skill of night-time navigation. Because of all these powers, I have only a few predators, and am able to think calmly and clearly in battle.

I will need to end this here. I have a training session scheduled in an hour, and I need to get to the other side of the rocky shore for the best patch. I'd booked it a week in advance to prevent wasting any time loitering around and chinwagging with the other folks there. I consider that sort of thing terribly counterproductive. If I get this role, I'd like to just keep my head down, quite literally, and just do my work.

Yours in regard,
Cone Snail.

APPLICATION FROM THE HERMIT CRAB

Hello, Hello ji

How are you? All fine, I am hoping? Family and all also, well?
This is Hermit Crab, this side.
I am here to apply to the Superhero Team you are all making.
You know, we have a lot in common, you and I.
We're also having huge populations on the beach. We cannot go five steps without bumping into each other.
Like you, we have a constant struggle with our houses. We're literally dragging our homes along the intertidal zone, and changing them constantly. We are ambitious like you, aren't

we? Always looking to grow. So we have to be aware of real estate opportunities. We have a nice deal — home on the beach, am I right? If you are looking, I have a very strong network within your kind also. I can find you something.

I know what you are thinking, if we're so alike, then why have me in the team?

I know the intertidal region and my network is stronger than the chiton's teeth also, you know? I know everything that is happening — who is looking for a house, who is vacating their shell, who is going around with whom, who needs protection from new predators, who is making babies — I know everything. See, I know some people will say, he's not even a true crab and all. But I ask you, what is in a name or species if I can do the job. The world needs inclusion and less judgement.

And boss, I get things done. If sea star needs a publicity campaign, I can put together a press conference in under an hour. If limpet needs a new algae patch, I get it done. I even helped that lefty snail find a lefty life partner — very proud of that one, I am. It's not easy, *haan*?

You know how everyone has been saying in their letters that they know a guy?

I am that guy.

Even the great octopus needs me to find her new entertainment when she's bored. Have you spoken to her yet? You should get her for sure for this. Actually, get 100 of them and you won't need anyone else. What a woman. What a mind. *Damn*. Okay, sorry, sorry.

You can just ask anyone about me.

All roads lead to me.

Say my pranam to your family.

Yours in hopefulness,
Hermit Crab.

APPLICATION FROM OCTOPUS

To
The Superheroes Council,
Aka
The Democratic People of the Marine Realm
AKA

A fancy name for you, the reader.

Hello darlings.

To be clear, right off the bat, I am not *applying*, I am *suggesting* to you a route that might be better for you. I don't really care if I make the team or not.

It's the principle of the thing.

I mean, you've read 200 pages of this book, and I've been watching the process. (Saw me watching? No? Think about that.) I can do almost ALL of the things the other creatures can do. Perhaps better. Honestly, just ten cephalopods would be more than enough for this. But you are including a large spectrum of often overlooked shore animals. I like the idea of diversity, so good job with that.

Although Hermit Crab tells me Sea Star's applied. I knew, of course; that one's not going to miss a single chance.

I am not going to sell my abilities to you. If you're smart enough and have done your homework, you'll know about them already. If you don't, there's no way I would answer to someone that foolish.

We're built for a life as a superhero. It is a wondrous thing that we're here and not on another planet, but to be honest, do you really know we don't commute? To hire us, you'll need to first find us, despite the camouflage and all. Oh, but you don't know so much yet, even with your little marshmallow tests, and your skin colour experiments. No one knows what my real body colour is, and I am glad because all these are just labels.

I must of course confess that as creatures with a superior level of intelligence, we bore very easily. So please consider an 'octopus entertainment person' for our time with you in your budget. I reckon hundreds of candidates will fall over themselves for this position.

So let us know. Or not. I don't care either way.

Yours in nonchalance,
Octopus.

APPLICATION FROM SCORPIONFISH

Hello people who decide for Superheroes team,

I am a scorpionfish but that's only if you see me. Most of the time you'll only feel me, by which time it will be too late, won't it? See these spines? They're loaded with venom. You step on us, and WHAM! Do you understand venom? I hear that snakes and spiders on the land around you have some.

Anyway, I change colour, so I can hide, like a tiny little mine in the middle of the intertidal zone. And imagine many of us — that would be a minefield, wouldn't it?

I am thinking I can be a good spy, a collector of information, see?

You know how there are these rocks that become meeting points for animals? I can be one of those, and they won't even know it. I can be still for hours. Hours. When I move, I can be both slow and fast. I am extremely adaptable. Basically, since no one knows my true personality, I can become whoever you need me to be! That's like the definition of a spy, isn't it?

I look forward to your positive response. I have another offer from a children's party organization, but I would much rather do this. The chance of lawsuits might be too much there, I mean, what if a kid annoys me and I impale it? Accidentally, of course.

Um. So let me know.

Scorpionfish.

APPLICATION FROM MANTIS SHRIMP

Hello,

Oh, I wasn't bowing like that, that's just how my hands are. That's why the name. You didn't need to . . . okay.

Awkward.

Anyway, I am the Mantis Shrimp, and I think I'd make a good addition to the Superheroes team under consideration. I am not too great with all these words and all, so I'll keep this short. I am very popular in my neighbourhood—they call me 'Mantis bhai'. Everyone in my tide pools (that is, the ones I frequent) knows my name, and they know whom to come to for any help. I don't get into politics and all. It's just me and my sunglasses and a cruise around my areas, new clothes to wear and food to eat and people to help and vermin to hit. Bas, that's all.

I mean, there are simply too many so-and-sos in the water and we've got to protect ourselves, and at the same time, find a way to eat and survive. In doing so, I have perfected two ways which I think might be of interest to you.

Some of my kin can spear the crap out of things, which is to say, impaling things is really good for our strategy.

The rest of us use brute force. I can clobber my way through anything you put in front of me. Really? Can you open a bivalve with your hands? Didn't think so.

I can punch the lights out of something small and even creatures as large as an octopus. There's a viral video of our fight online. Check it out: he beat such a hasty retreat, but I didn't let him off easy. I made sure he wouldn't go looking for trouble with my kind again. Fool. He thinks he's so cool, and intelligent. Well, he can put as many puzzles in a line as you can give him, but when it comes to it, I knocked him out, didn't I?

Anyway, this isn't about him.

I am strong. I am dependable and some of my kind have vision that is going to blow your mind (this is disputed).

So, let me know.

Yours in strength,
Mantis Shrimp.

APPLICATION FROM SEA STAR

Hello good people of the voting democratic,

First, let me apologize that this letter comes after the deadline. But I was finishing the publicity tours for my new book and motion picture. They just announced it last month; I am sure you saw it all over the news. Children just adore me, and I had to stay back at a few places for photos and autographs.

Of course, I told them I am not doing this for the publicity, but they just wouldn't listen. Oh my God, the applause I received for my book reading—you'd think I was the only star in the whole world!

Well then, I am sure you will consider me for this team even if I am a teeny bit late. I mean, it does need a little star power, eh? We all know who's actually going to open a few doors for the funding — it's not like you have a dolphin or whale in the team to do that for you. You don't, do you? I'd need the same contract as them if you do.

But, but but but — I am not just a pretty face, even if the photos tell you differently. You all saw me grow back an arm in the immensely popular 'The Star Diaries' and then literally growing back from an arm in 'Sea Star — The Return'.

Well, I have to rush, I have an appointment for a dinner date that someone's won in a contest. I don't mind it really, and it's always fun to see their faces when I literally upchuck my stomach on to my food, partially digest it outside the body, and then sip it in. A nice little party trick; I'm always such an entertainer! It's just better than chewing, and I can keep chatting all the while too. No bad chewing photos or anything.

The flatworm can do this too, by the way — poor guy has literally no room to actually keep solid food. Flatworm, little-known species. Follow them on Instagram. I honestly watch them to put myself to sleep sometimes — they're so fluid and graceful. So that's my good deed for the day, shedding light on creatures that are less fortunate, and away from the limelight. I'll tweet about it to my millions of followers too.

So, off I go. Can't keep my date waiting. My people will talk to your people.

I've enclosed a package with all my books, and photos from my latest shoot, all signed for you and your family. You're welcome.

Yours in stardom,
Sea Star.

REFERENCES

Introduction

Buxton, Orfeu M. et al. 'Sleep Disruption due to Hospital Noises'. *Annals of Internal Medicine*, 157 (3), August 2012.

Gorvett, Zaria. 'The Missing Continent It Took 375 Years to Find'. *BBC Future*, February 2021. Available at https://www.bbc.com/future/article/20210205-the-last-secrets-of-the-worlds-lost-continent?ocid=fbfut.

Hadhazy, Adam. 'Why Does the Sound of Water Help You Sleep'. *LiveScience.com*, January 2016. Available at http://citeseerx.ist.psu.edu/viewdoc/download? DOI=10.1.1.671.1334&rep=rep1&type=pdf.

Hazlett, B. A. 'The Behavioural Ecology of Hermit Crabs'. *Annual Review of Ecology and Systematics*, 1981.

Mehta, Sejal. 'Shore in the City'. August 2018. Available at https://indianexpress.com/article/express-sunday-eye/shore-in-the-city-5322445/.

Popova, Maria. 'How to Disappear: The Art of Listening to Silence in a Noisy World'. *The Marginalian*, Newsletter 2019. Available at https://www.themarginalian.org/2019/10/14/gordon-hempton-silence/.

Rotjan, Randi D., Jeffrey R. Chabot, and Sara M. Lewis. 'Social Context of Shell Acquisition in *Coenobita clypeatus* Hermit Crabs'. *Behavioral Ecology*, 21(3), 2010: 639–646.

Tricarico, Elena and Francesca Gherardi. 'Shell Acquisition by Hermit Crabs: Which Tactic Is More Efficient?' *Behavioral Ecology and Sociobiology*, 60(4), 2006: 492–500.

Chapter 1

Ang, Hing P. and Leslie J. Newman. 'Warning Colouration in Pseudocerotid Flatworms (Platyhelminthes, Polycladida). A Preliminary Study'. *Hydrobiologia*, 383(1), 1998: 29–33.

Behrens, Roy R. 'Revisiting Abbott Thayer: Non-Scientific Reflections About Camouflage in Art, War and Zoology'. *Phil. Trans. R. Soc. B*, 364, 2009, 497–501. Available at http://doi.org/10.1098/rstb.2008.0250.

Black, Riley. 'The Giant Squid: Dragon of the Deep'. *Smithsonian Magazine*, 21 June 2011. Available at https://www.smithsonianmag.com/science-nature/the-giant-squid-dragon-of-the-deep-18784038/.

Boynton, Mary Fuertes. 'Abbott Thayer and Natural History'. *Osiris*, 10, 1952: 542–55. Available at http://www.jstor.org/stable/301824.

Brown, Culum, Martin P. Garwood and Jane E. Williamson. 'It Pays to Cheat: Tactical Deception in a Cephalopod Social Signalling System'. *The Royal Society Publishing*, 2012. Available at https://royalsocietypublishing.org/doi/10.1098/rsbl.2012.0435.

'Decorating Crabs'. *The Science Teacher*, 85(1), 2018: 14. Available at http://www.jstor.org/stable/44843487.

Gilmore, R., R. Crook, and J. L. Krans. 'Cephalopod Camouflage: Cells and Organs cf the Skin'. *Nature Education*, 9(2), 2016: 1. Available at https://www.nature.com/scitable/topicpage/cephalopod-camouflage-cells-and-organs-of-the-144048968/.

Kever, Jeannie. 'Researchers Draw Inspiration for Camouflage System from Marine Life'. 18 August 2014. Available at https://uh.edu/news-events/stories/2014/August/0818Cephalopods.php.

McLay, C. L. 'Camouflage by the Masking Crab, Notomithraxursus (Herbst, 1788) (Decapoda: Brachyura: Majidae): Is It a Decorator or a Dressmaker?' *Journal of Crustacean Biology*, 2020. Available at https://academic.oup.com/jcb/article-abstract/40/6/673/5920554.

Meryman, Richard. 'A Painter of Angels Became the Father of Camouflage'. *Smithsonian Magazine*, April 1999. Available at https://www.smithsonianmag.com/arts-culture/a-painter-of-angels-became-the-father-of-camouflage-67218866/.

Millott, Norman. 'The Covering Reaction of Sea-Urchins I. A Preliminary Account of Covering in the Tropical Echinoid *Lytechinus variegatus* (lamarck), and Its Relation to Light'. 1955. Available at http://citeseerx.ist.psu.edu/viewdoc/download?doi=10.1.1.603.6386&rep=rep1&type=pdf.

Stangl, Paul. 'Geographic and Discursive Wanderings of San Francisco's "Evil" Octopuses'. *Interdisciplinary Literary Studies*, 18(3), 2016: 343–71. Available at muse.jhu.edu/article/629985.

Talas, Laszlo, Roland J. Baddeley and Innes C. Cuthill. 'Cultural Evolution of Military Camouflage'. *Philosophical*

Transactions of the Royal Society B: Biological Sciences, 372(1724), 2017: 20160351.

Torma, Franziska. 'Snakey Waters, or How Marine Biology Structured Global Environmental Sciences'. In 'On Water: Perceptions, Politics, Perils', edited by Agnes Kneitz and Marc Landry, RCC Perspectives, no. 2, 2012: 13–21.

Wallen, Martin. 'The Light Magic of Squid'. April 2021. Available at http://oceans.nautil.us/article/686/the-light-magic-of-squid.

Whalen, Andrew. 'Why Are These Sea Urchins Sporting Cowboy and Viking Hats? There's Science to Their Hot Looks'. *Newsweek*, 2020. Available at https://www.newsweek.com/sea-urchin-hats-saltwater-aquarium-cowboy-viking-top-hat-3d-printing-1500500.

Yu, C. et al. 'Adaptive Optoelectronic Camouflage Systems with Designs Inspired by Cephalopod Skins'. *Proc Natl Acad Sci USA*, 111(36), 2014: 12998–13003. DOI: 10.1073/pnas.1410494111.

Chapter 2

Estes, James A. et al. 'A Keystone Ecologist: Robert Treat Paine, 1933–2016'. *Ecology*, 97(11), 2016: 2905–09.

Mehta, Sejal. 'Creatures from Mumbai's Shores and Their Housing Stories'. May 2019. Available at https://india.mongabay.com/2019/05/creatures-from-mumbais-shore-and-their-housing-stories/.

Takeda, Satoshi, Masatoshi Matsumasa, Hoi-Sen Yong and Minoru Murai. '"Igloo" Construction by the Ocypodid Crab, *Dotilla myctiroides* (Milne-Edwards) (Crustacea; Brachyura): The Role of an Air Chamber When Burrowing in a Saturated

Sandy Substratum'. *Journal of Experimental Marine Biology and Ecology*, 198(2), 1996: 237–47.

Chapter 3

Bull, J. J. 'Sex Determination in Reptiles'. *Q. Rev. Biol.*, 55, 1980: 3–21.

Schlesinger, A. et al. 'Sexual Plasticity and Self-Fertilization in the Sea Anemone *Aiptasia diaphana*'. PLoS ONE 5(7), 2010: e11874. Available at https://doi.org/10.1371/journal.pone.0011874.

Chapter 4

Atoda, Kenji. 'Pedal Laceration of the Sea Anemone, Haliplanella luciae'. Publications of the Seto Marine Biological Laboratory 20, 1973: 299–313.

Cary, Lewis R. 'A Study of Pedal Laceration in Actinians'. The Biological Bulletin 20 (2), 1911: 81–107.

Hardt, Marah J. *Sex in the Sea*. Princeton University Press, 2015.

Palumbi, Stephen and Anthony Palumbi. *The Extreme Life of the Sea*. Princeton University Press, 2015.

Ruppert, Edward E., and Robert D. Barnes. *Invertebrate Zoology*. Vol. 6. New York: Saunders College Publishing, 1994.

Schlesinger, A. et al. 'Sexual Plasticity and Self-Fertilization in the Sea Anemone *Aiptasia diaphana*'. PLoS ONE, 5(7), 2010: e11874. Available at https://doi.org/10.1371/journal.pone.0011874.

Scales, Helen. *'Spirals in Time': The Secret Life and Curious Afterlife of Seashells* Bloomsbury, 2015.

Chapter 5

Lala, R. M. *For the Love of India: The Life and Times of Jamsetji Tata.* Penguin Books India, 2006.

'Sands of Time: The Innovative Spirit of Jamsetji Tata'. Tata Central Archives Newsletter. Available at https://www. tatacentralarchives.com/documents/Vol-XII,Issue-3-2015. pdf.

White, Mathew P., Ian Alcock, Benedict W. Wheeler and Michael H. Depledge. 'Coastal Proximity, Health and Well-Being: Results from a Longitudinal Panel Survey'. *Health & Place,* 23, 2013: 97 – 103.

Chapter 6

Allison, Peter A. et al. 'Deep-Water Taphonomy of Vertebrate Carcasses: A Whale Skeleton in the Bathyal Santa Catalina Basin'. *Paleobiology,* 17(1), 1991: 78 – 89. DOI: 10.1017/S0094837300010368.

Barber, Asa H., Dun Lu and Nicola M. Pugno. 'Extreme Strength Observed in Limpet Teeth'. *Journal of the Royal Society Interface,* 12(105), 2015: 20141326.

Blair, Steven et al. 'Hexachromatic Bioinspired Camera for Image-Guided Cancer Surgery'. *Science Translational Medicine,* 13(592), 2021.

Chhapgar, B. F. *Marine Mammals of India.* New Delhi: Oxford University Press, 2006.

Devries, Maya S. et al. 'Stress Physiology and Weapon Integrity of Intertidal Mantis Shrimp Under Future Ocean Conditions'. *Scientific Reports,* 6(1), 2016: 1 – 15.

Franklin, Amanda M., Matthew B. Applegate, Sara M. Lewis and Fiorenzo G. Omenetto. 'Stomatopods Detect and Assess

Achromatic Cues in Contests'. *Behavioral Ecology*, 28(5), 2017: 1329–1336.

Gamillo, Elizabeth. 'Enormous Prehistoric Marine Worms' Lair Discovered Along Sea Floor'. *Smithsonian Magazine*, 26 January 2021. Available at https://www.smithsonianmag.com/smart-news/enormous-prehistoric-marine-worms-lair-discovered-along-sea-floor-180976831/.

Göransson, Ulf, Erik Jacobsson, Malin Strand and Håkan S. Andersson. 'The Toxins of Nemertean Worms'. *Toxins*, 11(2), 2019: 120.

Greco, Patti. 'True Crime Stories Are More Popular Than Ever — Why Are We So Attracted to Them?'. *Health*, 29 October 2020. Available at https://www.health.com/mind-body/true-crime-why-we-love-it.

Hagan, John. 'The Pleasures of Predation and Disrepute'. *Law & Society Review*, 24(1), 1990: 165–177.

Safford, Matt. 'A Mantis Shrimp Inspires a New Camera for Detecting Cancer'. *Smithsonian Magazine*, 3 October 2014.

Scales, Helen. *'Spirals in Time': The Secret Life and Curious Afterlife of Seashells*. Bloomsbury, 2015.

Chhapgar, B. F. *Marine Life in India*. Oxford, 2006.

Schulz, Joseph R., Alex G. Norton and William F. Gilly. 'The Projectile Tooth of a Fish-Hunting Cone Snail: Conus Catus Injects Venom into Fish Prey Using a High-Speed Ballistic Mechanism'. *The Biological Bulletin*, 207(2), 2004: 77–79.

Chapter 7

Bonnet, David D. 'The Portuguese Man-of-War as a Food Source for the Sand Crab (*Emerita pacifica*)'. *Science*, 103(2666), 1946: 148–149.

Carbone, M., M. Gavagnin, M. Haber, Y. W. Guo, A. Fontana, E. Manzo, G. Genta-Jouve, M. Tsoukatou, W. B. Rudman, G. Cimino, M. T. Ghiselin, and E. Mollo. 'Packaging and Delivery of Chemical Weapons: A Defensive Trojan Horse Stratagem in Chromodorid Nudibranchs'. *PloS One*, 8(4), 2013. https://doi.org/10.1371/journal.pone.0062075.

Chhapgar, B. F. *Marine Mammals of India*. New Delhi: Oxford University Press, 2006.

Mehta, Sejal. '"Waterproof Fish": Look beyond the Venom of These Monsoon Visitors to Indian Beaches'. August 2018. Available at https://scroll.in/article/890111/waterproof-fish-look-beyond-the-venom-of-these-monsoon-visitors-to-indian-beaches.

Nusnbaum, Matthew and Charles D. Derby. 'Effects of Sea Hare Ink Secretion and Its Escaping-Generated Components on a Variety of Predatory Fishes'. *The Biological Bulletin*, 218(3), 2010: 282–292. Available at https://www.ncbi.nlm.nih.gov/pmc/articles/PMC2920541/.

Sheppard-Brennand, Hannah, Alistair G.B. Poore, and Symon A. Dworjanyn. 'A Waterborne Pursuit-Deterrent Signal Deployed by a Sea Urchin'. *The American Naturalist*, 189(6), 2017: 700–708.

Tindle, J. and P. Tadi. 'Neuroanatomy, Parasympathetic Nervous System'. *StatPearls*, Treasure Island (FL): StatPearls Publishing, January 2021. Available at https://www.ncbi.nlm.nih.gov/books/NBK553141/.

Chapter 9

Abrahams, Mark V. and Linda D. Townsend. 'Bioluminescence in Dinoflagellates: A Test of the Burglar Alarm Hypothesis'. *Ecology*, 74(1), 1993: 258–260.

Chapter 10

Boettiger, Alistair, Bard Ermentrout and George Oster. 'The Neural Origins of Shell Structure and Pattern in Aquatic Mollusks'. *Proceedings of the National Academy of Sciences*, 106(16), 2009: 6837–6842.

Rath, R., Saroj Kumar, and P. C. Naik. 'A Study on Acoustics of Conch Shell'. *Current Science*, 2009: 521–528.

Scales, Helen. *'Spirals in Time': The Secret Life and Curious Afterlife of Seashells*. Bloomsbury, 2015.

Chapter 11

Blanchoud, Simon, Buki Rinkevich and Megan J. Wilson. 'Whole-Body Regeneration in the Colonial Tunicate *Botrylloides leachii'*. *Marine Organisms as Model Systems in Biology and Medicine*, 2018: 337–355.

Carnevali, M. D. Candia. 'Regeneration in Echinoderms: Repair, Regrowth, Cloning'. *Invertebrate Survival Journal*, 3(1), 2006: 64–76.

Chhapgar, B. F. *Marine Mammals of India*. New Delhi: Oxford University Press, 2006.

Coe, Wesley R. 'Regeneration in Nemerteans'. *Journal of Experimental Zoology*, 54(3) 2005: 411–459.

Dupont, S. and M. Thorndyke. 'Bridging the Regeneration Gap: Insights from Echinoderm Models'. *Nature Reviews Genetics*, 8(4), 2007: 320.

Egger, Bernhard, Robert Gschwentner and Reinhard Rieger. 'Free-Living Flatworms under the Knife: Past and Present'. *Development Genes and Evolution*, 217(2), 2007: 89–104.

Gordon, Tal et al. 'And Then There Were Three . . .: Extreme Regeneration Ability of the Solitary Chordate *Polycarpa Mytiligera*'. *Frontiers in Cell and Developmental Biology*, 9, 2021: 793.

Gurtner, Geoffrey C., Sabine Werner, Yann Barrandon and Michael T. Longaker. 'Wound Repair and Regeneration'. *Nature*, 453(7193), 2008: 314–321.

Mashanov, V. S. and J. E. García-Arrarás. 'Gut Regeneration in Holothurians: A Snapshot of Recent Developments'. *The Biological Bulletin*, 221(1), 2011: 93–109.

Thorndyke, Michael C., Wei-Chung Chen, Philip W. Beesley and Marco Patruno. 'Molecular Approach to Echinoderm Regeneration'. *Microscopy Research and Technique*, 55(6), 2001: 474–485.

Williamson, Jane E., Stephanie Duce, Karen E. Joyce and Vincent Raoult. 'Putting Sea Cucumbers on the Map: Projected Holothurian Bioturbation Rates on a Coral Reef Scale'. *Coral Reefs*, 40(2), 2021: 559–569.

Xu, C., J. Palade, R. E. Fisher, et al. 'Anatomical and Histological Analyses Reveal That Tail Repair Is Coupled with Regrowth in Wild-Caught, Juvenile American Alligators (*Alligator mississippiensis*)'. Sci Rep, 10, 20122, 2020.

Zattara, Eduardo E. et al. 'A Phylum-Wide Survey Reveals Multiple Independent Gains of Head Regeneration in Nemertea'. *Proceedings of the Royal Society B*, 286(1898), 2019: 20182524.

Chapter 12

Bertness, Mark D. and George H. Leonard. 'The Role of Positive Interactions in Communities: Lessons from Intertidal Habitats'. *Ecology* 78(7), 1997: 1976–1989. Available at https://doi.org/10.2307/2265938.

Kalra, Aditya and Devjyot Ghoshal. 'Twitter Becomes Platform of Hope Amid the Despair of India's COVID Crisis'. 21 April 2021. Available at https://www.reuters.com/world/india/twitter-becomes-platform-hope-amid-despair-indias-covid-crisis-2021-04-21/.

Kandasamy, Kathiresan. 'How Do Mangrove Forests Induce Sedimentation?' *Revista de biología tropical* 51, 2003: 355–359.

Karplus, I. L. A. N. 'The Association between Gobiid Fishes and Burrowing Alpheid Shrimps'. *Oceanography and Marine Biology*, 25, 1987: 507–562.

Mehta, Sejal. 'Creatures from Mumbai's Shores and Their Housing Stories'. May 2019. Available at https://india.mongabay.com/2019/05/creatures-from-mumbais-shore-and-their-housing-stories/.

Ord, Terry J., Thomas C. Summers, Mae M. Noble and Christopher J. Fulton. 'Ecological Release from Aquatic Predation Is Associated with the Emergence of Marine Blenny Fishes onto Land'. *The American Naturalist*, 189(5), 2017: 570–579.

Raihani, Nichola J. and Redouan Bshary. 'Why Humans Might Help Strangers'. *Frontiers in Behavioral Neuroscience*, 9, 2015: 39.

Saenger, Peter, Ragavan Pandisamy, Chiou-Rong Sheue, Jorge Lopez-Portillo, Jean Yong and Mageswaran Thangaraj. *Mangrove Biogeography of the Indo-Pacific*, 2019. DOI: 10.1007/978-3-030-04417-6_23.

Schnytzer, Y., Y. Giman, I. Karplus and Y Achituv. 'Boxer Crabs Induce Asexual Reproduction of Their Associated Sea Anemones by Splitting and Intraspecific Theft'. *PeerJ*, 31 January 2017. DOI: 10.7717/peerj.2954.

Soni, Paroma.'"One Cup of Kadak Chai": How Mumbai's Koli Women Survived the Coronavirus Pandemic'. 13 March 2021. Available at https://scroll.in/article/989295/one-cup-of-kadak-chai-how-mumbais-koli-women-survived-the-coronavirus-pandemic.

Chapter 13

Aggarwal, Mayank, and Sahana Ghosh. 'IPCC Report Warns India Likely to See More Extreme Weather Events'. *Mongabay*, 11 August 2021. Available at https://india.mongabay.com/2021/08/ipcc-report-warns-india-likely-to-see-more-extreme-weather-events/

De, K., S. Sautya, S. Gaikwad, A. Mitra and M. Nanajkar. 'Characterization of Anthropogenic Marine Macro-Debris Affecting Coral Habitat in the Highly Urbanized Seascape of Mumbai Megacity'. *Environmental Pollution*, 2022. DOI: 10.1016/j.envpol.2022.118798.

Fairchild, Tom P., Mike S. Fowler, Sabine Pahl and John N. Griffin. 'Multiple Dimensions of Biodiversity Drive Human Interest in Tide Pool Communities'. *Scientific Reports*, 8(1), 2018: 1–11.

Kennedy, Emily et al. 'Biomimicry: A Path to Sustainable Innovation'. *Design Issues*, 31(3), 2015: 66–73. Available at http://www.jstor.org/stable/43829335.

ACKNOWLEDGEMENTS

Writing this book was a bit like being in a reality show. Some days were full of beauty, learning and a deep gratefulness for the opportunity to get to know the intertidal ecosystem so intimately. On other days, all my feelings were actively trying to destroy each other, all at once, without any provocation. As soon as I sat down to write, it was like the cameras came on and they would automatically become the worst versions of themselves and remind me that with no academic background in the sciences, I was woefully ill-equipped and should just drop the whole thing and run away to the mountains.

But then I read the late B.F. Chhapgar's *Marine Mammals of India* and *Shore Life of India* which are astounding collections of science communication. He writes, quite sternly, to my delight, 'The marine world is not the sole prerogative of the technically trained', giving me the confidence I needed to write this book. To all the people who agree with my reality show demons, please refer to this OG who says of scientists who might find technical flaws in his work that they should 'remember that they are in some measure to blame for not writing such a book themselves'. I laughed out loud at that and felt the now-familiar regret that I did not know enough to meet Chhapgar Sir when he was alive. There were threads and analogies in my mind that matched what I later read in his book, and that gives me no small amount of delight. All his books are masterclasses in how science can be communicated and felt. In the same vein, I hope readers understand that the science of these creatures is ever-evolving. New research might lead to different names for species and fresh insight into their lives after this book's publication.

To the other authors, I must bow for merely ensuring I read enough non-fiction to last me several lifetimes: *Sex in the Sea* by Marah J. Hardt, *Spirals in Time* by Helen Scales and my absolute favourite, *The Extreme Life of the Sea* by Stephen and Anthony Palumbi, who write about the ocean as some form of musical symphony. I also returned to Bill Bryson intermittently, as I always do, to remind myself that the only way I know of to cope with life's most serious questions is through humour. I hope this book makes you smile.

For the scientists who spoke to me, all the ones in this book and the ones whose papers I quoted from, the science communicators online whose videos I watched and the photographers who brought the shore life so much closer.

To all the projects that came my way, which allowed me to delve deeper, notably Inhabited Seas, a multidisciplinary project that sought to reimagine the futures of a coastal city. It brought me closer to scientists, researchers, architects and professors who shared their wealth of information with me.

To the journalists, activists and cartoonists who made the intertidal corner so much stronger by their dogged inclusion of coastal stories (shout-out to Rohan Chakravarty of Green Humour for making tigers and the intertidal creatures equals on the conversation and conservation panels).

To the original (and evolving) gang of Marine Life of Mumbai volunteers—Pradip Patade, Siddharth Chakravarty, Hetal Doshi, Jessica Luis, Deep Kanakia, Sayee Girdhari, Sagar Rajpurkar, Omkar Bhurke, Nikhil Sathe, Vighnesh Samel, Gaurav Patil, Sarang Naik, Fatema Hirkani, Sudarshan Pawar—thank you for walking the shore with me. See what it came to.

To Harshal Karve and Vardhan Patankar, for generously giving me their time and access to experiences and for fact-checking the book with Shaunak and Abhishek. So, if you have any problems with this book, you know who to send a stink bomb to.

To Shaunak Modi, for being a solid pillar, a hard critic and cheerleader as the occasion called for, with whose insight I was able to create the outreach that mattered over the years. He painstakingly and with harsh feedback saw the book through from its clumsy draft phase to what it is now.

To Abhishek Jamalabad, who introduced me to the marine life of Mumbai, and who encouraged and delighted in science storytelling across genres, who writes beautifully, and who allowed himself to be drained by my anxieties and insecurities while writing this book, no matter what time of day or night. Thank you for knowing the answers to my questions, and for allowing me to steal from your experiences and sometimes even your words. I will wait for your books to charm the world.

To my fabulous editor Manasi Subramaniam, who marvelled with me over emails and photos, and gently and skilfully steered the book to where it is today. To the entire team at Penguin Random House India (shout-out to Gunjan for his patience and understanding despite terrifying deadlines) for taking the book and swimming with it.

To all the people who allowed me to write from their homes over time when I couldn't find my words. The safest havens with laughter, food and love—Manish Mutalik and Shalini Singh; Urvi Purohit; Devang and Tatsat Munshi and the whole family, the entire G Gang for their loving support; and Punam Medh (who also, with calm logic and visual tools, helped me overcome a terrifying mid-book obstacle). Special mention to Zoya Tyabji who opened her gorgeous house to an almost stranger.

To all the friends and cousins, teachers and editors who have known I had stories to tell and told me to step up until I did. To those who dust out the demons so my words come out of hiding—Supriya Sharma (also for literally making this book happen), Pracheta Sharma, Sukanya Venkatraghavan, Nitasha Gaurav (and the Ladylords), Asma Kazi, Arushi Mehta. To Reshmi Chakraborty and P.S. Bhawana for listening to me rant throughout the writing of this book, for discussing the craft with me, for staying online and writing with me on video calls when I was stuck. To those that discussed and examined wordplay with me over the years, and those who inspired an understanding of the wilderness—Abhijit Dutta, Tushar and Mitai Shukla, Sudhir Rao, Bhavna Menon. To those who regularly keep me in their prayers—Gopi Patel, Kanan Chavda, Ami Shah. To the tiny windows of fun and food in the midst of the pandemic when I was tripping all over the words that were locked in for two years, Sonali and Shivani Shah and the Mehta girls. (If I have forgotten your name, you know that about me, too, and will forgive me.)

To my family, Mumma (for sharing her faith), Vaibhav and Mansi, for their acceptance of a writer's brain, constant support and belief. That sort of safety net is a blessing.

To my nieces, Aarya and Meera, who love without question and who with their tremendous energy, youthfulness and curiosity made the writing of this book bearable during the worst health crisis the world has seen in recent times.

And finally, to all of you, who love our coasts, who I might have met on shore walks, and those who I spoke to on my explorations. To the man who brought a small table and chair to watch a game of tennis on the shore while his wife went on her daily walks. To the man moved to tears on a video call while showing his family back home the vast ocean behind him. To the fisherfolk who spoke with me; to the people who conduct their businesses there; to the ones who play there, who bring picnics, who have dates there, who work there; to everyone who treats the shore with love.

Thank you.

Scan QR code to access the
Penguin Random House India website